George Halstead Boyland

Six Months under the Red Cross with the French Army

George Halstead Boyland

Six Months under the Red Cross with the French Army

ISBN/EAN: 9783337254377

Printed in Europe, USA, Canada, Australia, Japan

Cover: Foto ©Suzi / pixelio.de

More available books at **www.hansebooks.com**

SIX MONTHS

Under the Red Cross,

WITH THE

FRENCH ARMY.

BY

GEORGE HALSTEAD BOYLAND, M. D.,

Ex-Chirurgien de l'Armée Française.

CINCINNATI:
ROBERT CLARKE & CO.
1873.

DEDICATION.

TO

MONSIEUR M. FERDINAND DE LESSEPS,

IN GRATEFUL REMEMBRANCE

OF MANY KINDNESSES,

THESE PAGES

ARE MOST RESPECTFULLY DEDICATED,

BY

THE AUTHOR.

PREFACE.

During the siege of Metz, I found many leisure moments, and improved them by taking notes upon passing events, and writing an account of my personal experiences and adventures as Assistant Surgeon-Major in the "Army of the Rhine." They were made upon bits of paper; on my shirt-cuffs; in the lining of my képi, etc.: at times on the field of battle; at others while sitting on the floor of the barrack hospital, or reclining in my tent. They are composed without any pretension to literary merit, and are a simple statement of the facts told in my own language: as such I have the honor to place them before the public.

CONTENTS.

CHAPTER I.

Geneva Convention and "Sanitary Commission"—First French Ambulance—Departure from Paris—Nancy—Arrival of Wounded Turcos from the Battles of Reichshofen and Spicheren................... 1

CHAPTER II.

Barbarous Nature of Turcos—Arrival of German Prisoners—Exciting Scenes—The Nancy Ambulances—Disturbances between our Men and the Inhabitants—Orders from Headquarters at Metz.......... 23

CHAPTER III.

Breaking up Camp—Prussian Scouts in the Vicinity of Pont à Mousson—Arrival at Metz—Arrest of a Spy—Picket Firing—Flight of Napoleon—Marshal Bazaine...................... 29

CHAPTER IV.

Battle of Borny—The Mitrailleuse—A Detachment of our Ambulances on the Field—Villa of Borny—My Saddle-strap is cut by a Ball—Wounding of Dr. Good—In Search of the Missing.................. 36

CHAPTER V.

Retreat of the Third Corps and Guard—Evacuation of the Villa—The Train of Wounded—Armistice—Appearance of the Field after the Battle—Horrible Sights—A Violation of the Armistice and its Consequences... 44

CHAPTER VI.

Deserted Village—Dead lying in the Streets—Ambulance Wagons—Arrival at the Prussian Medical Headquarters—Battle of Rezonville—A Volley from the Bushes—The Farm of Moscow.......... 52

CHAPTER VII.

Firing upon our Ambulance by the Enemy—Abandoning a Wagon, Horse, and Material—Maison Rouge—The Regiments on the Hill—Attacking a Prussian Train—Men and Horses falling—The Commencement of Gravelotte... 60

CHAPTER VIII.

Incidents in the Battle of Gravelotte—Imprisonment of an American Citizen—Arrest of Schull—Grand Rout of the French Army—My Horse is shot under me.. 68

CHAPTER IX.

Dressing the Wounded in Châtel St. Germain—Neglect of an amputated Soldier—Lessy—I sleep in a Church surrounded by Dead—Arrest—Blind Man's Buff—The Prefecture and Jardin Fabert... 76

CHAPTER X.

The Emperor's Bed—Organization of our Ambulance and Régime for the Siege—Bazaine's First Sortie—Burning of Noiseville....... 84

CHAPTER XI.

Asleep during Action—The Ambulance shelled—Progress of the Siege —Foraging Expedition... 92

CHAPTER XII.

A Night with the Grand Guard—Privations—Death and Disease make Havoc among the Besieged—Metz "Sanitary Commission"—"Franc-Tireurs" 100

CHAPTER XIII.

Firing on the White Flag—The Garde Nationale—Grand Review—Interview with Marshal Bazaine—French Officers and Soldiers—Prussian Discipline.. 108

CHAPTER XIV.

Convent of the Sacré Cœur—The Convent Ambulance—Management of the Wards at Jardin Fabert... 116

CHAPTER XV.

Exposure of Wounds to the Air—Failing of Salt and Chloroform—The Consultation—Report of the Municipal Council—Skirmishing. 124

CHAPTER XVI.

In Front of Fort St. Julien—The Fight—A Shell explodes between Dr. Good and Myself—Struck by a Clod of Earth—Wounding of one of our Horses—Monitor Locomotives—Woippy........................... 131

CHAPTER XVII.

Village of Woippy—Horrible Scenes—Charge of the Prussian Cavalry—The Wounded—Infernal Machines........................... 138

CHAPTER XVIII.

The Trenches—Napoleon's Portrait by a Prussian Artist—St. Agathe—The Tobacco Factory turned into an Ambulance—Fate of the Wounded—Marshal Bazaine 145

CHAPTER XIX.

The Polish Prisoners—Prussian Rations—Proclamation with Reference to Flour and Wheat—The Hotel de Ville—Demonstration by the National Guard—Cries against Bazaine... 152

CHAPTER XX.

Speech on Behalf of the National Guard—A Visit to Café Infortuné—The Execution—Our Party are fired upon................................. 159

CHAPTER XXI.

Fooling the Guard—The Bogus Wounded Man—Extracting a Ball—Death and Disease—The Army of Relief............................. 166

CHAPTER XXII.

Entertained by the German Pickets—The 80th of the Line—A Night in the Elders—The Signal Lights—Morning—A Brush—Return of General Boyer... 173

CHAPTER XXIII.

Reply of the Prussians—Eating the Last Horses—Execution of Schull—A Medical Envoy to the German Lines—Firing upon and Wounding of the Same.. 180

CHAPTER XXIV.

Lying in the Rain and Mud—French or Prussian—A Narrow Escape—Horse-meat giving out—Brutal Butchery—Revolting Scene—The Last Meeting—Ordered to Fort Quelen...................................... 187

CHAPTER XXV.

Wounding of Second-Assistant Brière—No more Gas—Silence and Sorrow—Liberation of Mr. Eustis—An Excision of the Elbow by M. Liégeois—Distress 194

CHAPTER XXVI.

Last Resources—Capitulation of Metz—Protocole and Appendix—Riotous Scenes—Intervention of the Military—An Officer in Despair blows out his Brains—The Final Effort—A French Soldier's Knowledge of his Musket—Inspection of our Ambulance preparatory to the Surrender.. 201

CHAPTER XXVII.

Bazaine takes Leave of the Army—A Traitor and his Accomplices—Arrival of the Prussians at the Porte Allemande—The Surrender—Marching into the Enemy's Lines—Their Medical Service—They patrol Metz................ 209

CHAPTER XXVIII.

Triumphal Entrance of the Prussian Army into Metz—Troops passing through—The German Medical Department take Possession of our Ambulance—Our Surgeons leave for Belgium—Dr. Good and Myself bid Farewell to Metz—En Route for the Army of the Loire—Scenes along the Way—Arrival at Gland.. 216

CHAPTER XXIX.

The Murderous Attempt at Gland—We kill one and wound three—Flight in the Darkness—The two Villeneuves—Our Arrest—Chatenay—The Runaway—Arrival at Versailles—We give our Parole—Chartres.. 224

CHAPTER XXX.

The Palace of Versailles turned into a Hospital—The Last Battle—Paris... 231

SIX MONTHS UNDER THE RED CROSS.

CHAPTER I.

Geneva Convention and "Sanitary Commission"—First French Ambulance—Departure from Paris—Nancy—Arrival of Wounded Turcos from the Battles of Reichshofen and Spicheren.

The excellent arrangements made by the "Sanitary Commission" for the care of wounded soldiers during the civil war in the United States, were not without their effect beyond the Atlantic; and, in 1864, deputies from the different states of Europe met in a convention at Geneva, to discuss the best manner of re-organizing the medical department, which was in a very deficient condition.

It was agreed that, in case of necessity, civil medical officers should be incorporated into the army, and that volunteer ambulances should likewise be formed to follow the troops and render assistance while in action, but more especially to establish temporary hospitals in the rear—a first dressing having been given by the regimental surgeon and assistants on the field of battle. It was further agreed that a red cross on white ground should be the hospital flag, and should be universally adopted; all bodies of men, wagons, etc., bearing said standard should be respected; while officers and men should wear upon the left arm a band of the same description six inches in width. This was often abused; and I observed that ammunition was frequently moved from place to place under protection of our flag.

The medical appointments of each regiment consisted of a regimental surgeon, a surgeon-major, two assistants, and four infirmiers to each battalion (a battalion contains one thousand men); three battalions making a regiment. The combined medical staff of a division (two brigades) formed the ambulance corps of that respective division. It was with these division ambulances that new officers and men were to be incorporated without being detailed to any particular regiment. The Convention of Geneva had established depots in all the principal cities and towns of Europe. Shortly after the declaration of war against Prussia, materials, such as clothing, bedding, lint, medicines, surgical appliances, etc., were poured by patriotic subjects into the French depots.

Marshal Lebœuf, minister of war, mounted the tribune of the corps legislatif, on the 18th of July, and pronounced before that assembled body the following words: "Gentlemen, we are ready not only to meet the Prussians, but all Europe." That the marshal was mistaken from a military point of view the result proved; in fact, he afterward confessed to Dr. Lefort, director of our ambulance, that he had been Napoleon's dupe, and was induced to make the statement in order to shield him. That the medical department was still less prepared to enter upon a campaign is not surprising; and the arrangements, bad as they were, it is but just to say, were due to the generosity and patriotism of private citizens.

The education of a military surgeon occupies two years at the medical college of Strasbourg, at the expiration of which term graduates become assistant surgeons in the regular army. Whether men with so short a medical experience are capable to take the field or not, we shall not here undertake to discuss; but simply state that all our officers, with the exception of the under-assistants, were *diplomes* of the Paris University, and many of them had been already some years in practice. The under-assistants had most of them been in the university for from one to three years, the full course occupying seven years.

On the evening of July 25, 1870, I signed papers at the Palais de l'Industrie, which was at that time the Paris headquarters of the "Sanitary Commission," as established by the Convention of Geneva, to serve as assistant surgeon-major, in the first French ambulance, for the entire duration of the Franco-Prussian war, then about to commence. After ten days' campaigning in the capital, we left on the night of August 4th by the Chemin de fer de Strasbourg; and 9 o'clock found us *en route* for the seat of war. Our campaigning in Paris had consisted in strolling the boulevards; visiting the various *cafés chantants* in the Champs Elysées, to hear the patriotic songs then in vogue; and lounging about the gardens of the Tuileries for the purpose of listening to the warlike strains of the Marseillaise. This national hymn had been suppressed during the Empire, and was now revived only in order to arouse the people against their dangerous enemies, the Prussians. Campaigning in Paris proved to be one thing, campaigning in the field quite another; and our ten days' experience gave us no idea of the trials and hardships that were in store for us. The American war of secession had already given me an insight into military life; but I must confess my astonishment, when informed by Quartermaster Roussel, that I was expected to sleep on the ground, and, in his own words, "à la belle étoile." Upon learning this, my high notions of what an officer should be, and should have, received a slight shock. We were accompanied to the station by M. Nélaton and Dr. Chenu, chief of the medical department.

A few minutes before 9 o'clock, M. Liégeois, surgeon-in-chief of the first ambulance, summoned all the officers, and the roll was called by the dim light of a lantern. Our force consisted of M. Lefort, director; M. Liégeois; four surgeons-major (among whom was one American, Dr. Good, of Kentucky); ten assistants-major; and twelve under-assistants. In addition to these we had seventy infirmiers, whose duty it was to carry wounded from the field of action, to act as nurses, and render all the necessary surgical and medical assistance. The surgeons-major and first assistants were mounted. Our material consisted of eight army fourgons; thirty horses; one hundred and fifty stretchers; twelve appliances, with two wheels each, on which wounded men might be pushed along with great facility; beside instruments, splints, bandages, compresses, etc., innumerable, including eight large double tents, on the new Larrey principle, which were to serve as temporary abodes for the wounded, until they could be sent to the rear, into more permanent hospitals. Our effective could take charge of three hundred wounded. A large crowd had collected to witness our departure, and the train moved slowly off amid the cheers of the throng and the flourish of bugles. The convoy was a very long one, owing to the baggage, and to the fact that a battalion of the 35th regiment of the line accompanied us. All the officers rode in first-class carriages: this I thought all right. Our destination was Nancy, where we were to await orders from head-quarters, at Metz. The journey from Paris to Nancy occupies, under ordinary circumstances, five hours, but it took us eighteen. All night long we were awakened by the songs and shouts of the soldiers and our men,

many of whom were very patriotic and very drunk.
We met several trains bearing wounded, and arrived in
Nancy at 3 o'clock on the following afternoon. On descending from the train we found a collation awaiting
us, of which we partook freely, having had nothing but
a cup of coffee and a piece of dry bread since the morning. It now began to rain heavily; and as it was already late in the day, we were allowed to sleep in the
freight station, instead of occupying the quarters that
had been assigned us in an open field, about one mile
from Nancy. This was our first night "in camp." At
10 P. M., it had stopped raining, and the sky was clear.
The freight station at Nancy is situated about one hundred yards from the passenger station, and consists of a
quadrangular shed, open at the sides and ends, with a
board roof, through which the stars seemed to twinkle
merrily at our discomfiture. On one side of this shed
was the railroad track; on the other was a vacant yard,
in which our baggage wagons were left, while the horses
were tied to the railing running between the posts that
supported the roof on that side. Most of the officers
had, in the cantine allowed to each of them by the government (the word "cantine" does not signify, as in our
language, a drinking vessel, but a small, regulation,
wooden trunk), a bed, consisting of an iron frame with
a piece of canvas stretched across it, supported at the
foot and in the middle by small legs of the same metal,
while the trunk which thus remained open, formed the
head. When not in use this frame could be folded together, and made to occupy the lid of the cantine. Unfortunately, mine having been ordered rather late, could
not be finished in time, and I was obliged to leave Paris
without it, taking instead one that had no bed. Thus
I already found myself left in the lurch. The only thing

to be done was to order one of our men to get me out a stretcher. While aiding him to put it together I had an opportunity of examining it, and observed that it was constructed upon the same principle as those used in the American army. Our task was soon accomplished, and, having dismissed the infirmier, I wrapped myself in my huge blanket, and laid me down to rest, but not to sleep: a rather disagreeable impression came over me just then, as the thought crossed my mind that a few days might suffice to bring me to recline upon a stretcher in a very different condition. Sleep was out of the question. My reflections alone would have sufficed to keep me awake; and if these had failed, I had the kicking and neighing of the large draught-horses belonging to our ambulance, tied only two or three yards from my feet, and the whistling and puffing of a locomotive, moving back and forth, all night long, just near my head, to fall back on. After tossing for some eight hours upon my would-be couch, I was aroused by the clear notes of the bugle pealing forth on the fresh morning air. Soon the sun appeared. Breakfast was served; again black coffee and white bread, which latter experience soon taught me was a great luxury. This over, orders to pack up were given; packing occupied some three minutes, and the men were already carrying our cantines to the baggage-wagons.

The officers then received permission to be absent in the town until 10 o'clock, the hour fixed for our departure. The town of Nancy is situated about 150 miles east from Paris, in the department of Meurthe, near the river bearing that name. It has about 60,000 inhabitants; boasts a cathedral of some antiquity, and an ancient palace. It is well laid out, and the streets are clean. In the center of the town is the Place Stanislas, renowned by its historical associations. As we arrived here we observed a great crowd of people, talking and running about excitedly, and, upon inquiring, found that the first dispatches from Reichshofen and Spicheren were just arriving. Although those were unfavorable, yet the sanguine French insisted that to lose *these* battles was only *ruse de guerre*, in order to allow the Prussians to enter their lines, and then surround them without, as they said, allowing one man to escape. On my way back to quarters, I purchased four sheep-skins, which I afterward sewed together in the shape of a bag. In this I passed many a night. The horses were already to the wagons, and our chargers being saddled, we mounted. At the word "march," the whole ambulance and train evacuated the freight station. Our fourgons and material generally had been an object of interest to many thousands while they were yet lying before the Palais de l'Industrie in Paris, inside of which several of our large hospital tents were constantly pitched; and now, as we rode in procession through the streets of Nancy, the people cheered, while ladies came to the windows to wave us a salute with their handkerchiefs. This was only a repetition of what had taken place along the Paris boulevards, and in fact through every station on the road from Paris to Nancy.

We were soon out of the town. Descending a slight declivity on the east side, crossing the canal, and proceeding about five hundred yards further, we entered upon an open field. This was our regularly assigned camping-ground. Here we pitched our tents. The scene was a busy one. Men unharnessing horses here; men driving down the tent-pegs there; some unpacking; others bringing water for cooking purposes; while the officers were superintending everything. Many of our infirmiers were old hands at war. Some wore medals on their breasts; one, especially (Paul), had served in Italy, Mexico, the Crimea, and China, and was now going through his fifth campaign. It is customary in the French army to give a medal to the soldiers after each war. Paul wore all the above-mentioned, in addition to the *medaille militaire*, which is only given for some deed of great brilliancy and valor. He was intelligent, obedient, and obliging, which soon gave him a promotion.

It took us some time to get established in our camp. The dinner hour passed—no dinner. This was a little too much: two days and no dinner. I now began to think that being an officer and wearing a uniform was not what it was cracked up to be, especially as I had left all my friends in Paris, and was thrown among Frénchmen, very few of whom had any sympathy with or could speak the language of an American. The sun was sinking in the west when we sat down to our frugal repast, the greensward serving us for a table. Two tin plates that I had in my cantine came into very good play here. These, with other indispensable articles, I had purchased out of the five hundred francs paid me as a *bonus* when the enlisting papers were signed. The other assistants had received a similar sum; the surgeons-major, eight hundred francs; under-assistants and infirmiers, two hundred and fifty francs each. Our rations consisted of boiled beef and potatoes, cooked in small cãldrons, from which every one was expected to help himself. After our meal, we proceeded to wash our own dishes, in the hope that we might have another opportunity of using them on the following day, which was by no means certain.

Twilight had now faded into darkness; and as the clock in the cathedral tower tolled ten strokes, the lights were put out, and we retired once more to rest. All was quiet. We occupied a long hospital tent, which was intended to hold fifty of the new Tucker beds for wounded. We had two hundred of these beds among our material. They could be disjointed, made to occupy but small space, and carried with great facility.

I had a comfortable night's rest, enveloped in my sheepskins. There was no noise, as upon the preceding night. The horses were tied to stakes some one hundred yards distant. Two of them broke their halters and escaped. We were unable to recapture them, owing to the darkness and our ignorance of the country. The field in which we lay was separated from a similar one by a lane, the other side of which Colonel Proetch occupied with ten batteries of artillery. At break of day the colonel and his batteries could be seen filing off across the country in the direction of Metz, where a few days later we had the pleasure of renewing our acquaintance with him.

On the afternoon of August 7th, a bearer of dispatches came from Nancy to announce the disastrous battles, Reichshofen and Spicheren, in true colors. The enemy were advancing into French territory, and Nancy was declared in a state of siege. Orders were at once issued to strike tents and retreat within the walls. Our new quarters were in the Academy, which looks upon the Place Leopold, a large park, about a mile long by five hundred yards wide. Halls and lecture-rooms were turned into sleeping quarters for the officers, while for the men tents were put up under the trees in front of the Academy. At about 4 o'clock the strains of martial music, together with the heavy tramp of soldiers, announced the arrival of Marshal Canrobert with his division, who had left the camp of Chalons the day before. The men looked tired and dusty, and seemed glad to bivouac upon the Place Leopold. Fires were lighted, and the soldiers made soup. All the rest of that afternoon the officers spent in sipping absinthe at the various cabarets. I am sorry to state that the men followed their by no means worthy example. Many of the latter were soon intoxicated. At 9 P. M. the roll of the drums and the rattle of accoutrements announced that the division of Canrobert was preparing to leave; and, a few minutes afterward, regiment after regiment marched off, with the kettle-drums beating in front, to which the thunders of the approaching storm seemed to serve as a bass. We were soon left the sole occupants of the park. Silence reigned; all was dark and dismal, the rain falling in torrents. As yet, no wounded had arrived. Surgeon-Major Good and First-Assistant Frémy, who had been sent forward in the afternoon for the purpose of reconnoitering, returned shortly after midnight, to inform us that a train bearing five hundred wounded was nearing Nancy. All hands were aroused, and immediate preparation made for receiving the wounded men. I was assigned fifty beds, which I aided our infirmiers to put together, covering some with oiled silk. On these were to be placed the more severely wounded. This was done in order to protect the bed and allow the blood and pus from the wounds to run off in brass vessels, placed conveniently for that purpose. Instruments were taken out, also bandages and apparatus; in short, everything necessary for instant use. Our task was hardly done when the wounded began to arrive. The report as to their number proved to be greatly exaggerated. They were brought to us on stretchers, carried by two men each. They were principally Turcos, and most of them were wounded in the back.

CHAPTER II.

Barbarous Nature of Turcos—Arrival of German Prisoners—Exciting Scenes—The Nancy Ambulances—Disturbances between our Men and the Inhabitants—Orders from Headquarters at Metz.

WHY the Turcos were wounded in the back was explained to us from their own lips. They told us in broken accents that at Reichshofen they had been ordered to take a battery at the point of the bayonet. They charged; and arriving a few yards in front of the battery they had fallen into a deep and wide ditch which the enemy had dug out. All hope was now lost, and endeavoring to extricate themselves and retreat, the Prussians poured a volley into their backs. It was with some difficulty that we could gather information from them, as they understood but little French, the language used in their regiments being Arabic, although the officers were Frenchmen. The barbarous nature of these men showed itself occasionally by such remarks as these: "I killed four of them," "I cut his throat;" and they would roll their bloodshot eyes fiercely and ask how soon they would be well enough to fight again. Their wounds were mostly slight and we gave them the *"pansement simple,"* consisting of charpie dipped in cold water, with compress and bandage. Some of them had received a first dressing, which they still carried when they came into our hands: this appeared tolerably well adjusted, and had evidently been done upon the field. The most severely wounded of this lot was the blackest negro I think it has yet been my good fortune to behold. He had received a ball: it had entered the *os sacrum* at the height of the upper *foramina*, and lodged in the bone just behind the *promontorium pelvis*. This had already been extracted and a mèche inserted. We examined his wound, dressed it, and gave him some coffee and a cigarette. The poor fellow showed his ivory, and seemed very grateful.

August 8. The rain still continues: after a night's hard work I am relieved for a few hours. A very small part of this I devote to making my toilette, by washing my face and hands at the town-pump, and combing my hair over the trough, the water in which served me as a looking-glass, to the amusement of several small boys and girls. No servants were allotted to us, and we were obliged to be well served by serving ourselves, or getting the men to do little things for us, giving them a compensation in return.

In the afternoon, reports reached us that McMahon with his corps was marching toward Nancy. Second Assistant de Mussey and I rode out as far as Luneville, the third village in the direction of Strasbourg; but discovering nothing, forded the Meurthe and returned.

Our encampment on the Place Leopold had now become the rendezvous of hundreds of idlers, who flocked thither to gratify their curiosity, and became such a nuisance that we were obliged to station guards to keep them back. The prefect of the Meurthe and the mayor of Nancy visited our ambulance, and seemed very well pleased with the way in which things were managed; but had they been impartial medical officers, they might have found room for improvement in our discipline. In the afternoon a train from Metz arrived, bearing many more wounded. With them were two prisoners—the one a Prussian, the other a Bavarian—with whom I conversed in their own tongue, being the only one present who could speak German; they were evidently much pleased at hearing their language once more, and informed me that our insignia were well known to them, and that we should not be fired upon by their troops. We were still talking together when a squad of French soldiers came up. The officer in command said, "We will not murder you as you do our prisoners" (an unjust accusation), and ordered them to get off the train. They descended, and bidding me adieu, with mournful countenances, were marched off to prison.

The wounded now began to pour into Nancy, and a civil ambulance was established in the station itself for those who were unable to undergo the fatigue of further transport. This was under direction of a surgeon belonging to the Nancy civil hospital, which, together with the military hospital, was already filled.

Later in the day a brigade of McMahon's army passed through. Both officers and men presented a care-worn and jaded appearance: when their convoy was ready to move on, it was with great difficulty that the officers could muster their men, and get them into the wagons. Loud complaints were made by the latter that they were badly led and not sufficiently well nourished. Some of them were so worn out that they could scarcely walk: the Sisters of Charity in attendance requested the commandant to allow them to remain at least for a few days until they should recover sufficient strength to rejoin their regiment; to this he turned a deaf ear, and caused his soldiers to be hurried to the train, which then proceeded towards Chalons.

That night an exciting scene occurred outside the doors of the railroad ambulance. A man, whose deportment was quiet and unpretending, aroused the suspicion of some Frenchmen loitering about. He was apparently about thirty-five years of age. To a few questions addressed him by one of the latter, he replied with but few words, whereupon they fell on him and beat him, the bystanders shouting, "A Prussian spy! a Prussian spy! Kill him! kill him!" and in their blind fury they would doubtless have put an end to his days, had not one of their number just at that critical moment recognized him as a very respectable and loyal citizen of Nancy. I believe he was subsequently attacked and barely escaped with his life. I left this scene only to witness another: that of some drunken soldiers quarreling with a woman whose shrieks were truly heart-rending. Not knowing what might happen next, I quietly slipped six cartridges into my Smith & Wesson revolver. I returned to the academy and to bed at $11\frac{1}{2}$ P. M.

We were now regularly installed, and the officers were assigned places at the table d'hôte of the Hotel de France. For this the Intendance paid, and our salaries remained whole, to be paid us on the first of each month as follows: Surgeon-in-chief, 1,000 francs; each surgeon-major, 500 francs; assistants-major, 250 francs; under-assistants, 150 francs; chief of infirmiers, 100 francs; infirmiers, 75 francs.

About this time we began to experience much trouble with our men, who became quarrelsome among themselves, and disrespectful to their officers. Many had only joined the ambulance corps in order to have light work and heavy pay; while others, we afterward observed, had enlisted to rob the dead upon the field of battle, to say nothing of the living with whom they were in daily contact. Several were imprisoned at Nancy; others we sent back to Paris under escort, to be tried and sentenced. This made vacancies in our ranks, and we were obliged to take a few recruits. These were not long forthcoming. The soldiers in the ranks receive five sous a day in time of peace, and ten in time of war, or fifteen francs a month. A comparison of the salaries paid the infirmiers with those paid the common soldiers, will doubtless account for the zeal with which such places were sought.

On the morning of the 10th of August, Dr. Piotrosky, secretary of the Paris medical department, arrived at Nancy to inspect our ambulance and make his report. This was done in company with Director Lefort and M. Liégeios. M. Piotrosky was not so easily satisfied as the prefect and mayor had been; however, having made a careful inspection, he returned to Paris the same evening. Apropos of quarreling, I may add that our officers got along with each other very well: of course there were little jealousies and slight differences of opinion, that always will happen when any body of men are thrown together; but anything like a serious difficulty did not occur, and their deportment was in general soldier-like and gentlemanly.

In France there is an ill-feeling existing between the soldiers, including all officials connected in any way with the army, and the people. This ill-feeling is of long standing, and the conduct of Napoleon III, on many occasions, did little to better matters. We had not much to do with or say to the inhabitants of Nancy. Whenever it was necessary for us to have dealings with them, they took no pains to conceal their dislike to us; and insulting remarks were often made, but always behind our backs. We had no further trouble with them, except that fights were constantly taking place between our infirmiers and the workmen of the town who were for the time being thrown out of employment. These brawls, of course, could not be easily prevented; but whenever any of our men were caught in them, they were always severely punished.

Why the inhabitants of Nancy should bear medical officers malice, I could never understand, especially as some of their sick were indebted to them for private visits made; for which they got nothing and asked nothing.

The town was now fast filling up with wounded. The Nancy branch of the "Sanitary Commission" was obliged to call on well-disposed citizens, who came forward and aided in the work that they alone were unable to accomplish. Many families opened their houses and received each a few wounded. They hastened to make our flag and hang it from their windows, thinking, doubtless, that when the Prussians arrived, which now, indeed, was not far distant, it would protect them. The three large tents that we had set up before the academy were now full, and one hundred and fifty more wounded had just been consigned to us. In order to accommodate these, we were obliged to have recourse to our other five tents, which we were about to command our men to erect, when a dispatch from headquarters at Metz arrived, ordering us thither at once. Nothing was left us but to hand over all our wounded to the Nancy ambulances. The chief of the military hospital was summoned, and the lists were formally placed in his hands.

CHAPTER III.

Breaking up Camp—Prussian Scouts in the Vicinity of Pont à Mousson—Arrival at Metz—Arrest of a Spy—Picket Firing—Flight of Napoleon—Marshal Bazaine.

As soon as our wounded were transferred to the proper authorities, we broke up camp. It took our men some time to get our baggage, tents, etc., from the Place Leopold on board the special train awaiting us at the station. The town of Nancy was at this juncture in a state of flurry and excitement that may be better imagined than described, and comparatively but little notice was taken of our departure. We left Nancy on the 11th of August, at $5\frac{1}{2}$ o'clock in the afternoon, without a single regret, although we had no serious cause of complaint.

Now began a long and tedious journey, second only to that we had performed from Paris. The journey towards Metz was, however, much more disagreeable, from the fact alone that we now had the pleasure of riding in third-class cars, ill at ease and crowded together, as but scant calculation had been made for our ambulance. Three hours' good steaming brings you to Metz from Nancy in time of peace; in time of war, alas, how different! It was long past one o'clock the next morning when our train came lumbering and poking into the Metz *gare*. All along the road we had been subject to delays without cause, during which the soldiers (or *pions-pions*, as they were jocosely termed), of whom we had but a company with us, would run from the train to brooks or ponds that happened to be in the vicinity, to wash externally; or, if we chanced to be in a station, they invariably sought the cabaret to perform internal ablutions.

When we arrived at Pont à Mousson, about twenty miles west of Metz, we were informed that five Prussian Uhlans had been seen scouting in that neighborhood, but, upon finding that they were noticed, had turned and fled to the north.

Shortly after leaving Pont à Mousson, a storm, which had been threatening all the afternoon, burst over us; the rain began to fall, and continued until we got to Metz. Through the carelessness of our infirmiers no covering had been thrown over the stretchers, which were wet through; and only a few of the under ones had remained partially dry. I pulled and tugged at one of these, slipping down in the wet and cursing my ill-luck until it came out. I then carried it on my shoulders to the passenger station, as it was impossible to get a man at that moment to aid me.

The convoy had stopped some distance outside the station, leaving us to shift for ourselves. Owing to the lateness of the hour, and the confusion attendant upon our arrival, none of the officers could get their cantines; and all were obliged to follow my example, and sleep as best they might in the waiting saloons, upon stretchers, chairs, benches, tables, etc. But a few hours remained before the dawn, and these I wished already past, as we lay there all cramped together in the badly ventilated rooms of the Metz station.

At daybreak I was up and astir, and stepping outside the building found myself in the midst of a vast camp— soldiers here, soldiers there, soldiers everywhere. The whole country seemed covered with tents, which presented a dark and dowdy appearance, owing to the rain that was still falling. The soldiers were making coffee; the officers buckling on their swords or rolling cigarettes as they appeared at the tent-doors.

Immediately before me were the high walls of Metz, which seemed remarkably void of cannon for a city in a state of siege. I did not see one. The entrance on that side of the city was the Porte Serpenoise, and through this wagons with grain and vegetables were at that early hour passing. Behind me was the open country; in the distance, Mont St. Quentin, a large hill commanding the western side of the city. The fort of the same name on this eminence was not even finished, but contained, however, a few guns. Several hundred yards to the north of this was the fort of Plappeville.

After our morning repast at the *Restaurant de la Gare*, we took up the line of march to our quarters. These were in the Caserne du Génie, or military barracks, an immense building three stories high and forming three sides of a square. It is situated near the walls—in fact it is the first building on the left as you enter. The railroad track ran through the gate along the side of the building to a large open place called the esplanade. Preparations were made for a long stay, and our arrangements accordingly.

We had not as yet found it necessary to use any of our operating instruments, the small pocket case carried by each of us having been sufficient. The first part of the day was spent in putting our things in order and inspecting the town. Of course all now had beds, but at night we found that we were not the sole occupants of them; others were there to dispute our right in a very forcible manner, and finally obliged us to apply the famous insecticide powder.

Metz, the capital of Lorraine, one of the richest and

most flourishing provinces of France, lies, as it were, in a bowl, and is almost entirely surrounded by hills, upon each of which is a fort: like the one above mentioned, these were in a state of incompletion that is almost incredible. The Moselle flows through the town.

There is little of interest in Metz except the arsenal. The town is a garrison for 30,000 troops: although it had been besieged, as yet it had never been taken, and hence received the name of "La Pucelle." France naturally looked with pride upon this virgin city, a stronghold by nature if not by art. On the left bank of the Moselle, close to the water's edge, lies the prefecture—a fine building of brown stone, the headquarters of the Emperor and his staff, the gates of which were decorated with groups of flags. These were not alone confined to the prefecture, but from nearly every window in Metz flags were flying; so that as you stood at one end of a narrow street, and looked through, it appeared as though an alcove of red, white, and blue arched the way.

The scene was one of great activity: cavalry riding about, infantry marching from place to place, and artillery rolling heavily over the rough stones. On the Place de la Comédie, in front of the theatre, was stationed a battery, and as I passed through I noticed the smiths working at their forges. Upon speaking with a sergeant, he informed me that they were Col. Proetch's men, and that many of their horses had lost shoes in performing the *étape* or day's march from Nancy. He also informed me that the colonel had received command of Fort St. Julien, on the east side of the city, which they were to enter that day at sunset.

August 13. We are now taking rations at the Grand Hotel de Metz, and can make no complaints as regards sleeping-quarters. Everything has been put in proper order, and we are ready to take the field at a moment's warning. The court of the Hotel de Metz is occupied by a large squad of infantry, and as we sit at table we can see them through the windows, cooking their dinner and chatting merrily together.

Dinner is served at twelve, after which we loiter about the court to smoke our cigarettes and drink our coffee. A spy is brought in. General Coffinière, commander of the fortress of Metz, was at that time making a suite of rooms in the *rez de chaussée* his headquarters. Thither the spy was brought. It would seem he had been noticed galloping from a wood near Metz, in the direction of Saarbrücken; had been pursued and arrested by the French *védettes*, who were now telling their story to the general. The unfortunate man could not speak one word of French. After General Coffinière had interrogated him, he was led off between two files of soldiers. As he passed out, one of the gendarmes standing there made the motion with his arms as if aiming a musket at him, in order to convey the idea that he was to be shot. The little party turned the corner, and I saw no more of them.

An hour later found me on the road leading to Strasbourg, my object being to devote some leisure moments to exercise. The weather was fine, and I extended my ride for four miles. On either side, as far as the eye could reach, were soldiers of all arms; and their tents, which were now dry and white, contrasted picturesquely with the green fields. The road on either side was lined with tall elm trees. The soldiers were off duty, and many sitting upon the ground playing cards and smoking, unconscious that ere twenty-four hours should pass some of them would be no more.

I had arrived at a little roadside inn, called the *l'Ange*.

Here a captain stepped up to me (my horse was at a walk), and saluting, he politely informed me that our lines ended there. In advance, stationed at intervals of two hundred yards, were the pickets. I expressed my desire to proceed to the utmost limits of the French lines. The captain objected, stating that if anything happened he should be blamed; whereupon I invited him to the inn, but this he seemed still less inclined to accept; and I turned back, remounting the hill that I had descended. From this I perceived about a mile distant what proved to be the Prussian Uhlans reconnoitering the country. Their appearance excited the curiosity of both soldiers and peasants. A few shots from our pickets sufficed to make them disappear. These peasants, I afterward observed, were allowed to go back and forth unmolested, and doubtless often gave information to the enemy.

That afternoon the Emperor gave Marshal Bazaine command-in-chief of all the forces in and about Metz.

August 14, Sunday. Since our stay here, we have had literally nothing to occupy us, but are destined soon to find employment. When recounting my ride of the day before at breakfast, all expressed their opinion that the enemy were advancing upon Metz. The fact that Napoleon had resigned his command gave rise to much comment among the higher officers of the army, who did not, even at that early date, hesitate to express a want of confidence in Marshal Bazaine.

At 8 A. M., the Emperor, in company with the Prince Imperial and grand staff, attends mass in the cathedral. His majesty was attired in uniform as a general of division; the prince wore that of a corporal of the guard. Returning to the prefecture, they breakfasted, and left almost immediately after for Longueville, a village distant about four miles, on the Verdun road. The whole party slipped off so quietly that very few knew anything about it, although the Emperor had posted in the streets a farewell address to the army, in which he said: "The enemy are at the doors of France, and I expect my soldiers to repel the invasion." Napoleon rode in an open barouche; his son sat beside him; on the front seat, Dr. Conneau. The equipage was drawn by four horses. In front rode a squad of cavalry; behind the carriage came the staff; another squad of cavalry brought up the rear.

Marshal Bazaine was now in comand of the entire force, numbering 170,000 men. This army was called the "Army of the Rhine," but why, I could not exactly make out, unless because the war was about the Rhenish provinces. From the windows of the Caserne du Génie I noticed some artillerymen working slowly at mounting a cannon on the western ramparts; while on the eastern side of the city were a few mortars and small pieces, but no siege guns. I suppose they considered the defective forts a sufficient protection. As I read these lines, written some two years ago, the want of preparation seems almost beyond credulity; and the French certainly deserve great credit for holding out as long as they did.

CHAPTER IV.

Battle of Borny—The Mitrailleuse—A Detachment of our Ambulances on the Field—Villa of Borny—My Saddle-strap is cut by a Ball—Wounding of Dr. Good—In Search of the Missing.

THE last few lines of the preceding chapter recall to my mind a fact that I deem worth mentioning. It is this: that while the French required twice or thrice the ordinary time to perform a journey by rail, the Prussians were running their troops down to the front, not only according to the tables, but often under time.

It was 2 o'clock in the afternoon, when a few shots reached our ears. The pickets were engaging. These were followed by a sharp musketry fire, and volley after volley now rolled out. The Prussians, coming briskly out of the wood which lies just beyond the village of Borny, two miles east of Metz, commenced a lively attack upon our lines. This was the commencement of the battle of Borny. According to Marshal Bazaine's own report, issued January, 1871, his troops were all, at this date, upon the left bank of the Moselle. The marshal wished to operate a movement by which he could march his troops across the Moselle, there cut off the communications with Paris, and meet the army of the Crown Prince of Prussia, who he knew was coming up. Early in the morning, about 2 o'clock, this maneuver was already commenced; and now, after a lapse of twelve hours, the greater portion of the army was already on the right bank of the river: but still several divisions were moving, and the streets and bridges were blocked by them. There only remained the Third army corps and the Imperial Guard. These were preparing to follow.

The Prussians, who were well informed as to what was passing, gave them battle. General Steinmetz was in command of this force, which belonged to the army of Prince Frederic Charles. It was impossible to recall any portion of those French troops that had crossed the Moselle. The Prussians had them, not only few in numbers, but at a great disadvantage, of which they made the best, by giving them a signal defeat.

The fighting done by the French could not have been better. This was their first battle, and their spirit and vim were admirable. One regiment in particular, the 6th of the line, marched into fire singing, "Mourir pour la patrie."

This battle, though a small one, was one of the most closely contested of the whole war; the French having but 80,000 men in the field, while the enemy numbered 100,000. I happened to be at the Porte Serpenoise when the firing began; and I at once mounted the bastion above the gate, from which a tolerable view of what was passing might be obtained. I could see the bombs rising in quick succession and bursting over our soldiers, who now poured a murderous fire into the enemy's ranks. The rattle of the musketry was interspersed with the booming of field-guns, and the whirr-r-r-r of mitrailleuses. This latter cannon is about the size of an ordinary six-pounder, and contains twenty-five small barrels, each of which throws a ball not much larger than that thrown by the chassepot. These barrels are incased in an iron tube, and the piece presents the same appearance as any field-gun. They are breech-loaders, and work on the same principle as the chassepot and needle-gun. There is a crank behind to move the mitrailleuse from side to side as the discharge is made, in order to mow the men down, as the French thought. 2,000 mètres is good range. They resemble somewhat the American Gatling gun, but are less scientifically arranged. Such instruments of destruction were known long ago to the Japanese, and were not so new as Napoleon imagined. He kept what he supposed was a great discovery very close, and had the mitrailleuse manufactured in secret at a private foundry in the valley between Châtillon and Mendon, about ten miles west of Paris. The whole affair proved a failure. The mitrailleuse made a terrible noise, but that was about all. In conversation afterward with Prussian officers upon this subject, they have more than once informed me that the gun does not scatter, and that men had been found among their dead with twenty-five balls in them; moreover, they had taken many, and considered them only fit to send to the arsenals as curiosities.

I was soon ordered from the ramparts, and repaired to the Caserne du Génie. Mounting to the roof, I obtained a still better view of the battle, and could see the red flames belching forth on all sides. Here again I was told to descend. Thinking it strange that we were not ordered out, I sought our surgeon-in-chief to report myself. He was standing in the large court below, and seemed equally surprised that he had received no commands for action from Director Lefort, who was absent. We inquired for him, and found that he was at the Hotel de Metz. Thither we at once repaired. Imagine my astonishment to find him quietly seated at table enjoying his late dinner. The battle had already been going on for at least half an hour. We asked for orders —none! He seemed much surprised that we should be so zealous, and said, good-naturedly: "There's time enough." M. Liégeois expressed his disgust in plain language, and, turning upon his heel, ordered me to follow him. We returned to the barracks, and mustered thirty of our men and eight officers; we took two wagons. Surgeon-Major Good was dispatched forward. We also took with us what material we could in the shortest possible time get into the wagons. Some of the men carried stretchers on their shoulders, and came after us on foot. Most, however, were in the fourgons.

At least another half-hour had elapsed; but we were now dashing through the streets toward the Porte Allemande. This we reached in a very few seconds, but found it shut, which caused additional delay.

The road we took was not the same as the one on which I was yesterday, but parallel to it at some hundred yards distant. This we followed for about one mile and a half. All along we were met by wounded soldiers, who were still able to walk, and were making their way back to Metz.

As we passed through the several farmyards, whose sole occupants were women and children, these came to the roadside in tears, evidently weeping for husbands or brothers in the army. The shells were now raining down upon all sides. Turning short to the left and crossing a meadow, and hurrying up a small hill behind which a detachment of cavalry were awaiting the order to charge, we entered the village of Borny, in which were stationed five regiments of the guard, a part of the reserve. Upon asking a colonel how the battle was going, he replied, in true French style, "We have won already."

The battle at this moment was not quite half over, it being 4 o'clock in the afternoon. Galloping through the dirty roads of Borny, we reached the other end of the village, and were now under full fire. We were with the right wing of the army, and immediately behind the attacking line. From this point we saw many falling upon all sides, while the bright red of their uniforms contrasted strangely with the great clouds of white smoke that rolled heavenward. The din and clash were rendered only more deafening by the groans of the dying and the shrieks of the wounded, many of whom were trampled under foot by the advancing columns, or stepped upon by horses whose riders had fallen.

M. Liégeois detailed me, giving me eight men, Surgeon-Major Martin eight, and Assistant-Major Lachapelle likewise eight. He, himself, with the remaining men and officers, returned to the village, saying that they would there establish the field-ambulance in a fine villa known as the Château of Borny, and dispatch a man to Metz for reinforcements.

The twenty-four men upon the field had twelve stretchers with them. Surgeon-Major Martin took command, ordering Assistant-Major Lachapelle to the left, myself to the right, while he took the center. I immediately went to work, and observing several fallen soldiers about one hundred yards before me, dashed there. We picked them up, four at a time, and sent them to the château, the men depositing them there, and returning for others. The shells were screaming over us, and the bullets whistling about us. While giving directions to one of my men, I felt a sudden sharp thud just at the back of my saddle, and, upon looking around, I saw that one of the straps that held on my blanket, which I always carried in a roll behind me, was cut by a bullet. My horse seemed to enjoy the battle amazingly, throwing his head back and forth, snorting, and pawing the ground. I moved about that part of the field, rendering all the assistance possible with my meager corps. As it was I succeeded in picking up fifty wounded in about four hours. No reinforcements came out to me, although the rest of our men and material had arrived at the villa. I thought it rather surprising that I should be thus left to take care of myself.

It was now evening; twilight had set in, making the flame from the cannon and muskets all the more lurid. The brisk fire that had been kept up all the afternoon, began to lag and was diminishing rapidly. The cannon had ceased; a battery of mitrailleuses, behind which I was at that moment, limbered up and was preparing to leave the field.

I may here state that this was the only breach-loading cannon the French possessed. The others were all very handsomely gotten up (as was also the mitrailleuse), being of brass, with pet names carved on them, and handsomely embossed; but all were muzzle-loaders. The Prussians, on the contrary, had *no* muzzle-loaders; and their guns, which resembled iron stove-pipes, were of cast-steel. They shot with great accuracy.

Soon the musketry dropped off, little by little, and the last shot was fired. Darkness had set in.

This field was the only one the Army of the Rhine occupied after battle; from all the others they were driven.

The Prussians having accomplished their object, namely, to interrupt Marshal Bazaine's movement, in order to allow the Crown Prince to come up, passed away to the north in the night, not, however, without leaving 30,000 men on this side in case of an attack by the French on the next day. Judging from the small force left, they seemed to be pretty sure no such attack would be made, and that our Third Corps and guard would cross the Moselle and regain the rest of the army.

In the silence that ensued shortly after the battle, we could distinctly hear the hurrahs of the victorious enemy, who were lighting their camp-fires and bivouacing. All along their lines the Prussian national hymn is sung, and an accompaniment played by the bands of the different regiments. Above, the stars are brightly shining; and the cool evening breeze springing up is very refreshing, after the dust and heat of to-day. I remained a minute to contemplate the scene. Presently the clatter of hoofs reached my ears, and Surgeon-Major Good rode up. I observed that he wore a handkerchief about his head, and, upon inquiring if he had been wounded, he replied, "A mere scratch—a ball grazed my temple." We returned together to the château, and I was happy to learn that this was the only casualty—if we except that the horse of Surgeon-Major Martin had shied and slightly bruised one of his men.

As we enter the flower-adorned gates of the cozy villa, a strange sight presents itself to our view. On either side of the road that winds from the gates up to the villa is a large grass plat. On this the wounded were lying in rows. Some were on stretchers, some on the ground; others less severely wounded sitting on the steps of the porter's lodge; others, again, leaning against the parapet of the villa balcony. The only light we had was that of a huge fire, built in the middle of the yard, and a few lanterns, which gave a very peculiar and grotesque effect to all that was passing. Those leaning against the parapet and sitting on the wood-pile had come off the best. These we dressed first, as being the most urgent. Their wounds were mostly about the arms and shoulders. Our men brought water from the well. I was of those attending to this batch. Dr. Lefort was engaged in examining some of the more severely wounded. We had a very active night of it, making incisions, extracting balls, washing, binding, etc. With our ambulance corps were two Catholic priests, who now went about giving what consolation was in their power to those unfortunate sufferers. After working hard until past midnight, we heard, while still in the middle of our duty, that a commandant of artillery had been left upon the field in a wounded condition. Two men and an officer were now called upon to volunteer to go out again upon the field and seek the wounded commandant. I offered my services, and having the choice of two men left me, named Paul and Jean. We took a stretcher, some lint, a bandage, a cup of water, and departed. We entered the field by the main road. After strolling about, inquiring of pickets and stragglers if they could tell us in what part of the field the wounded men lay (the line of battle having extended for over a mile), we stumbled upon a company who were lying down. The officer was standing up. No sentinels were out, and the officer cried, "Qui vive?" I answered "Friend," and told him my mission. He gave me no information, but advised me to follow the road that led in the direction of Courcelles.

CHAPTER V.

Retreat of the Third Corps and Guard—Evacuation of the Villa—The Train of Wounded—Armistice—Appearance of the Field after the Battle—Horrible Sights—A Violation of the Armistice and its Consequences.

ACTING upon this advice, I turned to the left, and soon reached the road, which I scoured well, but could find no traces of the missing man. At 1 A. M. we returned to the villa of Borny—a private villa, whose owner, with his family, had left since the arrival of the army. I am writing these few lines standing at the gate, in a little memorandum-book. During our absence several of the wounded have died; others are arriving; I am called and must close this.

. . . . . . When the wounded arrived we had no place for them: the villa, yard, and stables were all full—also one or two of the neighboring barns; and we were obliged to have recourse to the village church, just across the road. This was a small stone structure, with a heavy oaken door, studded with massive iron rivets. The sexton, who lived in a cottage hard by, had fled, and in his fright, taken the key with him. To tear rails from a fence, and commence battering at the church door was the work of an instant. A few good blows sufficed, and the door fell in with a great crash. We now put the fresh wounded into the pews and around the altar, having first scattered straw everywhere.

I noticed that the altar was bare—the silver candlesticks and chalice were gone. More of the wounded breathed their last here. The sound of soldiers marching at this moment reached our ears; going out to the door I saw the infantry of the Third Corps, to which our ambulance belonged, filing past: they marched in silence; the bright scabbards of the officers, who wore the hoods of their overcoats over their heads, and the smooth bayonets of the men, glittered in the moonlight. The retreat had already commenced, and all the troops that remained were on their way to rejoin the rest of the army. Soon the artillery came rattling along, while the cavalry brought up the rear. General Bourbaki, then in command of the Imperial Guard, had ordered the movement to be made without further delay. Our eight army fourgons, which were nothing more than the wagon in use in the American and Prussian armies (box-like and oblong in shape, with a top), could contain but 96 of the more slightly wounded—those who were able to sit up; and we had altogether 210 on our hands. We had no time to spare, and were rather put to it to know what we should do. We were not long deciding, however, and resolved to bring a sufficient number of horses and hayracks belonging to those inhabitants who still remained, into requisition. This took some little time, although it is needless to say that none of the villagers required waking up after the events of the day. They willingly gave us all the assistance in their power, and many gave blankets to the wounded, that they might not suffer during the journey to Metz, for it was now getting on toward morning, and was quite cold. The wagons, ten in number, each drawn by two horses, we filled with straw; this also the peasants willingly gave from their granaries. We placed the wounded carefully upon the straw, folded our stretchers, and joined the retreat. It was only two or three days later that I found leisure to write up all that passed on that, our first day in action.

Our ambulance train fell into the line of retreat behind the artillery. The fires that had a few hours before lighted the country far and wide, were deserted and smoldering; and as we rode back toward Metz, we were pushed and hustled about by the cavalry, who had came up and wished to pass us. The clock on the tower of the château of Borny struck three as we left the village. On the road we were often blocked, and at these times I had an opportunity of glancing around me; the cavalry were still pressing us hard, but we would not make room for them, and they were obliged to remain behind, which it was their place to do. The men were all very tired; and I could see the weary artillerymen every now and then drop their heads and lean down on their horses' necks, to catch a few minutes of sleep. We found troops breaking up camp all about that district. Soon all were gone, and only the dead remained behind in the village and on the field. Many of our wounded complained, but we could do nothing for them then, as we could not stop the column. The French wounded are generally conveyed from the field on "cacolets." These cacolets are very badly arranged; viz., a mule is harnessed with a large wooden saddle, on either side of which is an iron chair. Unfortunately these chairs move; and if the two wounded men who are to occupy them are not put up at exactly the same moment, the chair sinks on the side of the one that reaches it first: if, on the contrary, they are not taken down together, the one that is left receives a jerk and a shock that would be sufficient to throw a weak man to the ground. Moreover, every step the mule takes, jolts the wounded and gives them pain. A wounded captain, who was borne upon one of these, exclaimed to us, "For the love of God, gentlemen, take me down and let me die." We took the captain off and put him on a stretcher, after which he was quiet. These cacolets are provided by the French government. I consider them a very bad method of conveying wounded, and condemn them heartily. The chairs have a frame work of iron, and can be unfolded into a bed: I have tried them, and they are very uncomfortable, even for a well man. One of the best means of conveying wounded men is that which we were now putting into practice, namely, in hay-racks, half filled with straw: the jolting and shaking are thus avoided; and such racks can most always be obtained without difficulty, from the different villages or farms that now-a-days always lay in the track of an army. We had reached a lane connecting the two roads already mentioned: into this we struck, leaving the main column. This lane was free, and we quickly reached the Strasbourg road, by which we thought to gain the gates of the city in shorter time; but upon turning into this road, we were met by another column: these were chasseurs, and with them was a train of cacolets; one of these passing by, struck my leg, inflicting a severe bruise, which did not tend to better the bad opinion I had formed of them. Closing in, we joined the rest, and were again moving slowly toward the walls of Metz, that were now only a few hundred yards distant. Around the walls is a deep fossé, filled with water, and some fifty feet wide. As we crossed the wooden drawbridge, myriads of frogs set up such a croaking from the stagnant and filthy water (which doubtless did much to engender disease during the siege that followed), as was never before heard. A cavalry officer, riding beside me, said "they sang at being waked up so early." Just before us were a company of the dragoons of the Empress. The gates of Metz were closed, and the column halted: a blast from the *clairon's* trumpet caused the sleepy guard to get up. He opened to us, bearing a candle in his hand, and rubbing his eyes. I saw no sentinels anywhere about. The city was in a state of siege, and the enemy not three miles distant. Such gross neglect can not be too severely reprimanded.

After a slight delay we rode through the arched gateway into the fortress. Here the troops turned to the right, in order to follow the walls around to the Porte de France, and there cross the river. We left them, taking the streets through the middle of the town, whose sole occupants were occasional sentinels, pacing leisurely before government buildings. We rode into the barrack yard at daylight, just as the reveillé was being sounded.

August 15, 5 A. M. We are carrying the wounded into the caserne, and placing them in the beds, dividing the different rooms into wards; each of the four surgeons-major, together with two assistants-major, two under-assistants, and four infirmiers receiving charge of one ward. Our service consists of four rooms, containing each twelve beds. By 12 M. we have performed five operations in our ward alone, and given all a first dressing. Of these operations, two were amputations of the humerus at the upper third; one of the femur, at the upper third; one of the foot, according to Byrogoff; and one resection of the shoulder-joint. Of these, we lost but one; his blood being in a very bad state, pyæmia soon set in, and he died on the fourth day after the operation. Among all our wounded, during the campaign, the cases from this battle were the most successful, owing partly to the prompt manner in which they were treated, partly to the fact that the siege was not yet commenced, and fresh provisions could still be procured. Speaking of performing operations on the field of action, this was impossible, owing to the confusion that always attends an action and to our bad organization. If the wounded were borne to the rear and operated on within the next twelve or twenty-four hours, this was all that could be expected. The sooner the operation is performed, the better the chances of success. Among our operated was one in M. Gilette's service, both of whose tibias he had been obliged to amputate. M. Gilette told me that during the operation one of the Catholic priests came in and insisted upon giving the subject absolution. M. Gilette ordered him from the room. I later had an opportunity of judging of the bad effect of *this* system of allowing the priests to be present constantly with the soldiers, among whom were some Protestants; and these they would allow to suffer, and—it is stated on very good authority—even die, keeping food and other things from them, because they would not kiss the crucifix and acknowledge the Roman Church.

1 P. M. A lancer rides up to the caserne with a dispatch, to inform M. Lefort that the Prussians had sent a horseman, in the morning, to ask for a twenty-four hours' armistice, which had been accepted by the French. The object of this armistice was to return to us some of our wounded, and to give the génie on both sides time to bury the dead still lying on the field. We again leave the barracks, this time only leaving behind a sufficient number to take charge of the wards until we shall return. We are once more dashing along the Route de Strasbourg. We soon reach the field. The aspect is very different from yesterday. At first a few dead horses meet our eyes: further on, horse and rider are fallen together. The country about presents the appearance of a field of blood (the red on the dead French giving that idea), while the entrails of sheep, horses, cows, etc., are scattered about. Knapsacks, guns, muskets, sabers,

bayonets,—everywhere. Arriving a short distance from where the Strasbourg route forms a right angle with that leading to Courcelles, we make a halt, observing the Prussians moving about upon their portion of the field: above them floats the white flag with the red cross. On perceiving our train, one of their officers, with two men, advance. We likewise send an officer and two men from our number forward, to meet them. Observing what is passing, I gallop out into the field to see the *génie*, who are hollowing out long ditches within which to put the dead. They are unarmed, in accordance with the stipulations of the armistice.

As soon as the ditches are ready, the dead are picked up, each body by two men, and laid not overcautiously into their final resting place. This done, a Catholic priest walks the length of the grave, sprinkling it with blessed water, and all is over. One squad of dead in particular attract my attention: they all lie in a row in exactly the same position as when the fatal bullet arrived, showing that death must have been instantaneous. One is on his knee; another lying full length behind his knapsack, of which he had made a temporary breastwork—from beside this he was aiming; a third was in the act of throwing up his hands, as if just struck, while a piece of skull was broken in, and the protruding brain showed the cause of death; a fourth was still loading his chassepôt;—etc. The most interesting fact of all is, that every one of this squad, numbering some fifty men, were shot above the shoulders, the wounds being mostly in the head, some in the neck. This is a mark of great precision in shooting, and has doubtless been done by the German jägers, or sharp-shooters, who came out of the wood which skirts the otherwise wide and open field. While standing there, I see that all the knapsacks with which the field is plentifully covered, are broken open and empty. This had evidently been done by marauders, as the Prussians, with whom we afterward spoke on this head, were also of that opinion. At this moment a peasant, who had followed me through curiosity, picked up a chassepôt that had belonged to one of the dead, and pointing it in the direction of the enemy, playfully pulled the trigger; the musket that was still loaded went off. If at that moment the Prussians had opened fire and shot down our whole corps, not one word could have been said—we had violated the armistice. I got down from my horse, and giving him to one of the gènie soldiers to hold, I beat the man lustily with the flat of my sword, and then followed him across the field, administering kicks and blows as he moved away.

CHAPTER VI.

Deserted Village—Dead lying in the Streets—Ambulance Wagons—Arrival at the Prussian Medical Headquarters—Battle of Rezonville—A Volley from the Bushes—The Farm of Moscow.

THIS peasant came off better with me than he would have done with a sub-officer of the génie, who drew his sword and wished to kill him. Returning to my horse, I saw that our ambulance had turned the angle, and were now hurrying on down the Courcelles road. This road ran between two high banks, so that the wheels of the wagons and the legs of the horses were hidden—hence we named it "le chemin creux:" it bordered on the wood, and was exactly through the middle of the battle-field. It seems to have been the dividing line of the two columns' attacks: for on the right were our dead; on the left, those of the enemy. They lay in pools of gore. I noticed one without a head; another cut in two in the middle: this had evidently been done by a shell, for the wound was ragged, and not like that made by a saber. The upper part of the body was some twenty feet distant from the lower part, to which it was connected by the intestines, which were thus making almost a straight line from the *duodenum* to the *sigmoid flexor*. As we rode along the route, I noticed a dead soldier, who was lying upon his face at the foot of a rude stone crucifix, to which he had evidently been able to drag himself after being wounded, for I could follow the tracks of blood for some hundred yards back. Fresh graves were everywhere to be seen on the Prussian side—the only tombstone of some, being a saber driven into the ground; others had small crosses made from the branches of trees. The Prussians had been at work early that morning burying their dead, offering this as a proof that they had lost but few; they had not buried any of our men, although some were lying near the Prussian graves.

We were now in a valley, having passed through a dirty hamlet, which was entirely deserted, dead men lying about the streets. Here we are in the Prussian lines. The three Prussian medical men that had accompanied left us here, and we received in their stead a squad of Uhlans as escort. The large quantities of arms and helmets that were stacked gave us another proof of how active our enemies had been during the morning. In about ten minutes more we reached the château of Colombey, where the Prussian medical staff were installed. As we entered the yard, an officer saluted us politely, and invited us to alight. He spoke very good French, and seemed to take much pride in telling us that he had many French wounded in the château. Let me here state that in the battle of Borny we had taken no prisoners, and none of the enemy's wounded had fallen into our hands.

The château of Colombey was a beautiful private residence, containing fine pictures, choice statuary, etc. The grounds were handsomely laid out. The Prussians had made themselves pretty comfortable; and I could see that tables, bureaus, and étagères, for which they had no use, had been quietly dropped out of the windows. Private letters belonging to the family, who had fled, were scattered about. The best suite of rooms was occupied by the Prussian surgeon-major, while in all the others, as in the barns and stables, wounded were lying. Broken helmets and side arms were strewn about. A few dead French soldiers were lying before the stable. Behind the house itself was stationed a Prussian ambulance. An ambulance in the armies of Europe signifies a whole corps of medical officers and men, including the wagons, etc., and does not refer to the latter alone, as with us. The wagons in use in the regular French army for carrying the wounded from the field (in case "cacolets" do not suffice) are called "carts"—*charettes;* they hold only two men; have two wheels; a board bottom, with no springs. Over the whole is placed a canvas frame in hot weather. This affair is drawn by one horse, and makes a jolting and rattling which are very objectionable. They are but little better than the cacolet. I noticed, also, that the French regiments going into action were unprovided with lint and bandages, these being in the rear at the field ambulance. The little that an occasional surgeon, who happened to be with the troops in the line of fire, had in his small satchel is hardly worth mentioning. One of these surgeons in particular I several times noticed sleeping in the coffee-houses along the route, while he might have been rendering service at a moment when it was necessary to bring every recourse into play. This man was not the only French surgeon who had a taste for cafès and absinthe.

The Prussian surgeon in command at the château of Colombey—a large man, some six feet in height, with a grizzly beard—ordered his infirmiers to assist us. They and we then entered the barn. We found it filled with French wounded. It would be impossible to depict their joy as they saw their own uniform, and heard their own tongue once more spoken. The French soldier feels his captivity keenly, for, as a rule, he speaks no language but his own. We took them up one by one, and placed them in the wagons; and as each was filled, the commandant handed us a list, which we signed, returned to him, and then submitted ours for his signature. He made the wounded men swear upon honor not to serve again during the entire war.

Speaking of wagons, the best I have seen were those in use by the Holland ambulance that came into Metz after the siege: they were constructed more like the ambulance wagon in use in the American army, having four wheels and springs, with a good roof above. They could accommodate four wounded reclining, and eight sitting, and had a tank, from which water could be drawn when needed.

While we were yet at the château a small circumstance occurred, showing how well the Germans were acquainted with the surrounding country. One of our men being asked the distance from there to Metz, replied, "Four kilometres." "No," said the Prussian, "it is exactly six kilometres;" and he produced a map from his pocket, such as had just been issued to the grand staff of the French army only a few days before. While we were getting our train of wounded in order, a few of our men had been detailed to assist in burying the French dead, the few Prussian dead being carefully concealed in the bin of the stable.

While this was going on I stepped up to the trench. Just then one of our infirmiers threw up his hands and exclaimed, as he recognized his brother among the dead, "*C'est mon frère!*" This was very touching.

In going to our train of wounded that was now ready to start, I stumbled over the helmet of a dead Prussian. Stooping down I tore the brass eagle from it as a souvenir, and passed on.

We had some difficulty in starting, as we had again brought the hay-racks into requisition; they were driven by peasants. When the Prussian officer gave the word "Forwärtz," they did not understand, and he very kindly helped them with an oath and a push. The squad of Uhlans accompanied us back to the limits of their lines. Here they left us. Again we passed over the battle-field, and the setting sun cast its last rays upon the fresh mounds.

The French had no pickets anywhere; and the Prussian scouts were loitering all along our road as if they belonged there. I noticed one in a cabaret only half a mile from Metz.

August 16. Battle of Rezonville; ambulance stationed at Le Point de Jour; seventy-five wounded are brought up by our men, but we are obliged to retreat with the army, having first sent the wounded forward. The field remains in the hands of the Prussians. One of our men, Henri, while attempting to aid a wounded colonel to descend from his horse, received a ball in the intestines. Later they are both picked up and brought to our ambulance. The Point du Jour is a small farm just this side of Rezonville, consisting of a house and two barns. Our position on the field was generally between the column of attack and the reserve. Such was now the case. The farm-house and barn had already been loopholed by our soldiers, so that they might thus have a breastwork against the enemy. The retreat was sounded, and the reserve set fire to all the buildings of the farm.

We retreat a mile toward Metz. There we endeavor to establish ourselves temporarily in the open field, and planting a stretcher in the ground, fix the hospital flag to it. We were behind a small hill, and had dressed three or four fresh wounded, who, seeing our flag, had been able to reach it unaided. We are again obliged to move to the rear, as the French were falling back continually.

Reaching the church of Rozerieulles, I observed several soldiers standing before the door talking. Almost at the same instant I heard the crack of some half a dozen rifles, and look in the direction of the sound just in time to get a glimpse of a squad of Prussian cavalry dashing in among the bushes not five hundred yards distant. Two of the men had fallen; we hastened to pick them up. The surgeon-in-chief, thinking our quarters rather hot, ordered us further in. All that day we were unable to do much, as the troops were constantly driven back; we were obliged to go with them, and so could not find an opportunity to render very much effective assistance. We rode back to quarters at dusk, the firing having ceased, and many of our wounded having been left upon the field for the Prussians to pick up.

10 P. M. I walk through the wards and observe that several more have died during our absence. The wounded infirmier is placed in the surgeon-in-chief's ward, where he receives the best care. Upon examining his wound, we find that the ball has entered the umbilical region, exactly in the *linea alba*, and still remains in the wound. Any examination is attended with so much pain that we are obliged to renounce it. The only dressing we apply in this case is a compress, dipped in cold water. At 12 P. M. we turn in, leaving only the watches up.

August 17. The weather still continues fine. No renewal of the attack of yesterday, although picket-firing commenced at daybreak, and is still going on. The returns from the battle of Rezonville have not yet been handed in; they will doubtless be larger than those of Borny. Those of Borny (French statistics) are as follows: Killed, wounded, and missing on the Prussian side, 10,000; on the French side, 3,000.

Rezonville is situated on the west of Metz, and about four English miles, or twelve kilometres from the city. It is on the road to Verdun. Thus the movement of Bazaine to check the Crown Prince of Prussia in his march toward Paris is failing. Our soldiers are already tired.

The Third Corps and the Imperial Guard came up from Borny on the 15th. The Third Corps fought at Rezonville; the Guard did not.

At 3 o'clock this afternoon we are ordered to Maison Rouge, a small village just beyond Longeville. It was here that the Emperor was taking breakfast on the morning of the 15th, when a shell fell in the yard and burst, breaking the window of his bedroom. The next day passing along the Verdun road at a swinging pace, he just escaped being captured by the Prussian vanguard, whom he espied in time to spur on and make good his flight. That morning he arrived at Etain at 11 o'clock, and was taking his ease at the "Hôtel du Cygne," while the noise of the battle of Rezonville could be distinctly heard in the distance. These circumstances were afterward told me by the proprietor of the Swan while I was dining in the very chair which Napoleon had occupied.

Maison Rouge lies in the valley. I am ordered to ascend the hill, on the top of which is the plain of Gravelotte, in order to reconnoiter. The road here passes through a narrow defile, and is quite steep, hot, and very dusty. Emerging from the defile, it winds up the side of the hill, and then comes out abruptly on the plâteau, where I had now arrived. A train of cacolets is coming toward me. In this there are a few Prussian wounded. I ask the leader if there are any more wounded left behind; he replied, "Oh yes!—at the Ferme de la Moscowa [all the farms about that district bear such names as I have mentioned]." Taking him at his word, I turned about and was soon down the hill. When I arrived at Maison Rouge, I made my report to M. Lefort; he at once ordered the ambulance forward.

We pursued the road I had just taken, and were soon on the plâteau of Gravelotte. From where we now were the Ferme de la Moscowa was about three hundred yards to our right. We had come up a by-way, and the main road lay between us and the Ferme. This was filled with infantry. It was impossible to pass at that moment.

CHAPTER VII.

Firing upon our Ambulance by the Enemy—Abandoning a Wagon, Horse, and Material—Maison Rouge—The Regiments on the Hill—Attacking a Prussian Train—Men and Horses falling—The Commencement of Gravelotte.

THE retreating column was now blocking the route entirely, and moving slowly on. I could see the long road leading in the direction of Rezonville, Gravelotte being much nearer, and only two kilometres distant. The 13th Lancers were coming up—not in the regular column, but through the field in which we were waiting for an opportunity to proceed. Troops were to be seen in all directions, still moving. They seemed to bear to the north, in the direction of St. Privat. It was a pretty sight.

2 P. M. The sky is clouded, a slight breeze blowing; the sun appears at intervals. Frossard's division cross the plain, not far off; and their buttons and the barrels of their muskets shine in the sunlight. They enter the wood of Vaux, and disappear. The reserves are filing down the hill behind us, and only their bayonets are still visible, making a hedge on the border of the plain. We are completely surrounded by troops. Much remark is made about several of our commissaries, who came out to the field in hackney coaches. They are to be punished. We have been waiting for three hours for an opportunity to cross the road and proceed to the farm, which is within a stone's throw. Here again the French showed bad organization in not allowing the ambulance train to cross the road. The halt would have lasted but a minute. The wounded were suffering, perhaps dying;

and we were losing time, when every minute was valuable. At 3 o'clock we see the end of the column. At 3:30 we are able to cross the road, and draw up before the Ferme de la Moscowa. We enter; and, to our surprise, find that the wounded have been removed, if there had been any there: the sole occupant of the farm being a dead captain of the line, with a frightful gash across his head. Having purchased some bread and wine at the inn at Maison Rouge before leaving, we now commenced a lunch.

Hardly had we done so when a volley was fired at us by the Prussian pickets, about a mile off. Shortly after, the boom of a cannon announced that the enemy were pressing close upon us. On looking around, we perceived ourselves entirely alone. The Prussians had probably been unable to see our flags, two of which floated from small poles on the wagons, one on either side of the driver.

The wagons were unharnessed, and had been left under the trees, while the drivers, half intoxicated, were lolling about on the grass. The volley that had been fired was fortunately without effect on the men; however, one of our horses was hit. I do not need to tell that we were soon up and doing. In our hurry to leave the place we forgot several of our stretchers. The Prussians were now plainly visible among the trees on the other side of Gravelotte. Fearing a repetition of the fire, we dashed out into the open, leaving behind the wounded horse, also one wagon, which we never recovered. Our object in taking the open was to display our flag, which the Prussians could now easily make out, even without field glasses; and they did not renew the fire until we were at a distance. We pass off the plateau down the hill by which we had only a few hours before ascended, and soon reached Maison Rouge. Here a division took place: half of those that had come out were ordered back to Metz, the others were to remain, and, in case an attack should commence, which seemed very probable, to dispatch a messenger to Metz.

Immediately before Maison Rouge, and north of the main road, is situated a high hill, which is now covered with French troops. Thither I ascend with two men; the rest remain in Maison Rouge. The ascent was through a wood, and occupied some little time. Three regiments were encamped there. The top of this hill was bare, and as we jumped the fence which cut it off from the wood, three or four of the officers who were conversing just near, came up to demand the meaning of this intrusion. We explained that we were reconnoitering, and asked them if they had any wounded among their men. They replied, "No: our men have fought at Borny and Rezonville. We have lost many; but our wounded have all been sent to the rear." They were very polite, and entered freely into conversation, showing us about the camp. The arms were stacked here and there, without any particular attention to order. I have generally seen them stacked in rows. The soldiers were dirty and undersized. As usual, they were trying to amuse themselves; and some were cooking chickens that they had evidently stolen from the neighboring farms.

Their tents were also pitched here and there. One of these officers told me he was much surprised that he had not been wounded in one of the two battles, stating that he had counted over three thousand projectiles that had passed over his head.

The trumpets summon the men to roll-call. These trumpets were used upon every occasion. Drums were also beaten constantly, and such a din and clatter kept up, that had the enemy been deaf they must have heard them. This is the case throughout the whole French army. The Prussians are seldom heard until they are upon us like the whirlwind. From this position I could command the plain of Gravelotte, and see the enemy still behind the village. A train of the enemy is coming up to Gravelotte. Upon this a battery just in front of the camp opens a brisk fire. I see some of their horses hit, and the men fall from the boxes. The Prussians do not reply. The train soon disappears. To the left of this battery are two lines of infantry, firing in open order into the wood, into which I can see the Prussians running at the other end. The first line of this company is firing on their knees. This skirmishing lasted until dark.

August 18, 2 A. M. I am aroused from my sleeping-quarters, which are now in a vacant house belonging to the École d'Application. We have been obliged to give up our beds in the caserne to the wounded. M. Liégeois, in search of volunteers to go into the enemy's lines and receive some of our wounded, calls upon me; I get up. Dressing did not take long, as I had not had my clothes off for five days. Following M. Liégeois to the large place in front of the cathedral, I found four fourgons and ten men, some of whom carried lights, all ready to start. I had with me my second assistants, Vegû and Brière. M. Liégeois did not accompany us. I felt quite important, placed in charge of this train, which I ordered forward at once. Our destination was the village of Gravelotte. Passing out of the Porte de France, and crossing the Moselle, I struck into the Verdun road. I pressed the men on, as the Prussians had sent us word that all must be over by daylight. I had no difficulty in passing our lines, and still less in entering those of the enemy, who were on the look-out for us. As we galloped up to Gravelotte (we had four horses to each fourgon), I could see nothing but the dark outline of the houses. At the entrance of the village a Prussian officer of the medical staff rode up, and, after saluting, said: "The French ambulance, I presume?" I replied: "Yes: this is a detachment of the first French ambulance, Third Army Corps, under my orders." He then told me that there were thirty-eight French wounded in his ambulance, where they had been placed temporarily. He explained that they were from the battle of the 16th and the skirmishing of the 17th. I requested him to conduct me thither. It was in the village school-house. I was struck at once with the neatness of everything, and with the completeness of the arrangements. He assured me that he had been in Gravelotte since yesterday afternoon only, and yet three rows of beds, constructed from the benches and desks, seemed to make the wounded men much at ease. A petroleum lamp was hanging from the ceiling; this was well trimmed and burning. The windows were so completely darkened that outside of the house it was impossible to see a ray of light. This was to conceal their whereabouts. I asked him how he did about ventilation. He went to a window, lifted a piece of cloth which was suspended from the top, and showed me that it was open to a sufficient extent. The floor had evidently been swept out, as the water-traces left by the sprinklers attested. "These are your men," he said, leading me to one part of the room; "take them at once. Our forces are behind the village, which they must occupy at daylight. I, too, must evacuate. To-morrow we expect a great battle." He then called a dozen of his men to aid us. We soon transferred our wounded to the fourgons.

The first faint streaks of the approaching day had already marked the east when we rode away from the old school-house.

We bade the Prussian officer farewell and hurried forward. We were but a few hundred yards from Gravelotte, and had reached the last German pickets. They halted us. I told them my mission, and pointed to the flag. I saw that they were not the same ones that were there as we came. They saluted, and allowed me to pass on.

It was getting lighter every minute. Casting a glance behind me, I could see the main body of the Prussian army marching quietly up behind the village. There must have been at least 100,000 in that army. I could clearly make out the dark blocks of troops and the dull steel of their muskets.

Many regiments in the Prussian service have their musket barrels of unpolished steel. This has a double advantage. It does not rust so easily, nor does it reflect light and heat.

The road here bends, and we were now half-way between the French and Prussian lines. Knowing the eccentric habit of the French, their bad organization, and, moreover, that their pickets had been changed, I could not guarantee for our safety until we were so near that they could recognize us as their men. As I rode into our outposts I turned again, and now saw the Uhlans riding about in Gravelotte, while a Prussian battery was getting into position.

Our pickets would not wait until our train was at a distance, although I requested them to do so, but cried out, "There they are!" and opened fire. The Prussians, be it said to their credit, waited until we had disappeared under the brow of the plateau. I then heard a sharp skirmish commence. I reached the Caserne du Génie at 6 A. M. On making my report and handing the list of my wounded to the director, he gave fresh orders to proceed again in the direction of the firing. I had barely time to swallow a cup of wine. We were again on the road to Gravelotte. We found difficulty in making our way, as a brigade of the reserve was moving in the same direction. It was 11 A. M. before we reached the field. We took our stand behind the left wing, and began to make preparations for action. The skirmishing of the morning had dwindled down to an occasional shot.

We were only a few feet from the main road. We had not been there ten minutes when the diligence plying between Metz and Verdun came up. We halted it, and told the post-boys that a battle was about to commence, advising them not to proceed. But this, French-like, they seemed to take as a good joke on our part. However, they drove on, but did not go far, for about one kilometre beyond they were stopped by the Prussian pickets and turned back.

As they were again about to pass on, I saw them stop and a gentleman get out: a young woman, who happened to be walking toward Metz, got in. This gentleman now advanced in our direction, while the post-boys snapped their whips and hurried on.

He was a man of about forty-eight years of age, medium height, wearing a full gray beard and moustache. He was dressed in a traveling suit and wore leather leggings. As he came up, he raised his hat to me, who happened to be the first one he met.

I noticed by his accent, as he addressed me in French, that his mother tongue was English; and from his interrogation as to the skirmishing that had taken place in the morning, I took him to be an English correspondent.

"Oh, no!" he said, when I asked him: "I am Mr. Charles Eustis" (presenting his card), "of Boston." And he told me his story in a very few words. He was the Paris agent for Remington & Co.'s rifles, and had been sent by his firm to the front in order to offer the Remington musket to the French army. This struck me as rather peculiar, for the army had been in the field for at least two weeks, and it was not the moment to swap guns. I told him so. Well, he said he had come down to speak with Marshal Lebœuf on the subject, stating that he knew the marshal well personally. He had stopped at Nancy on business, but had been unfortunately arrested as a spy, and taken before Marshal Canrobert to prove his identity. After being liberated, he came down to Metz, nothing daunted. Now about this time, Schull, the great spy, who, at Strasbourg, had contracted with the French, receiving five thousand francs from them, had gone over to the Prussians, with whom also he did then or had previously stipulated. It seems that he it was who informed the Prussians that the French were few in number at Weissenburg, and thus caused their reverse at that point.

CHAPTER VIII.

Incidents in the Battle of Gravelotte—Imprisonment of an American Citizen—Arrest of Schull—Grand Rout of the French Army—My Horse is shot under me.

AFTERWARD this Schull had come to Metz under pretense of giving the French information about the Prussians, expecting thus to receive an additional sum. The French authorities, who had gotten wind of this, were on the look-out for him.

On the afternoon of August 14th, Mr. Eustis, who had just arrived, was walking upon the terrace of the Hôtel de l'Europe, when a man in citizen's clothes, who afterward proved to be one of the secret police, accosted him with, " You are Monsieur Schull—is it not so ?" " No," he replied, " I am Mr. Eustis." " Very well," said the other, " please to follow me ;" and the two crossed the street to the Hotel de Metz, just opposite. Gen. Coffinières was informed that his police had captured the great spy.

Mr. Eustis was now conducted before him, and had much difficulty in proving that he was really a citizen of the United States; for as ill luck would have it, Schull, who had lived in America, was also provided with a passport from that country. On Mr. Eustis' passport they read Charles (badly written) for Schull. Mr. Eustis said if they would send for Marshal Lebœuf he would soon settle the matter. The Marshal, although sent for, did not seem inclined to respond; and Mr. Eustis was taken down to bastion No. 110, and imprisoned in a casemate, being ill fed and suffering greatly from cold.

He was kept there until the morning of August 18th, when the real Schull was captured and Mr. Eustis liberated. Now, Schull was a German: he had been well educated, and had served under Maximilian in Mexico.

Mr. Eustis, as may be imagined, lost no time in pulling up stakes, and wisely concluded to take his place in the diligence *en route* for Paris *via* Verdun—the railroad communication was already stopped, the French having fired the bridge and torn up the tracks about twenty kilometres west of Metz.

We now see him before us after finding that he could not continue his journey—in the diligence.

I expressed sympathy for him, telling him that we were compatriots, and offering him any assistance in my power.

When being asked why he had not returned to Metz, he said he wished to see the battle. For this curiosity he paid dearly, as we shall presently learn.

The enemy now began throwing shells at our left wing; and soon battery after battery opened fire, while the infantry were engaging all along the line. The battle was commencing in good earnest. The line extended from about two miles south of Gravelotte north to Saint Privat. This battle was the greatest of the war—the Prussians having three hundred thousand men under fire, and the French one hundred and seventy thousand, or their entire force. To attempt to describe the scene is useless for me. Smoke and fire seemed to flash everywhere; from out of bushes, behind trees, and in the open field. I was ordered forward with a few men to direct them in picking up wounded and sending them back to our field ambulance. We were in the act of trying to raise a wounded major, whose fallen horse was still lying on him, when a bullet entered the brain of one of my men who was standing next to me. The skull was shattered in the temporal region. Death was instantaneous. We succeeded in rolling over the horse, whose side had been opened by the bursting of a shell, deluging the wounded captain with blood. The captain I placed on a stretcher, and had him carried back to the ambulance. I left our dead man on the field to be buried with the soldiers after the battle.

While still moving about in that part of the field, Second Assistant Brière came running up to tell me that the ambulance had been obliged to change quarters and move to the north, as the Guard Imperial had come up and wished to occupy our ground on which they might place a battery.

I ordered the men to follow, and galloped after the main body, who were already some distance off and proceeding at a sharp pace. They had already sent one lot of wounded to Metz, ordering the men to deposit them there and return with the empty fourgons. We did not halt until we had reached an open field opposite the village of St. Privat. We had scarcely arrived when Marshal Lebœuf with his body-guard rode past. M. Liégeois had some conversation with him, in which he said, "Our medical department is well organized."

This speech was but a repetition of what he had said some months before in the Corps Législatif at Paris; and any one who reads these pages will judge for himself whether the French medical department was well organized or not.

The Marshal saluted and moved on some four hundred yards, where he halted under a tree, got down from his horse, and consulted a map which he took from his pocket. After some minutes he remounted: all went on, and were soon lost to sight.

It was now 5 o'clock in the afternoon. The battle, which for an hour had been at its height, did not seem to abate. The right wing, where we now were stationed, had fallen back, leaving several large caissons of ammunition together in the open field. By some chance or intention a shell struck this, and there was a fearful detonation that shook the very ground on which we stood, as bodies of caissons, wheels, tongues, etc., flew into the air in a great black cloud.

About this time we saw the whole country alive with soldiers turning to flee.

A battalion of the Guard came up and formed a line in order to prevent this; but the retreating soldiers paid no more attention than if they had not been there, and rushed through them as if they had been made of paper. This Guard battalion had been commanded by their officer to fire. This they refused to do, saying, " We will not shoot our brothers." The Guard were now ordered to take part in the battle: this was the last resource. The band struck up the Marseillaise and marched boldly forward. They endeavored to edge a wood about half a mile distant and come out the other side, where indeed they arrived. Their object was to flank the enemy; but the Prussians, who seemed to have received reinforcements, literally decimated them with their artillery and infantry: after which, the famous cavalry charge took place. The Guard fled in disorder.

Finding ourselves closed in by the retreating army, we were obliged to turn and do likewise, having been unable to render any further assistance during the battle of Gravelotte.

Now ensued a complete rout. Cavalry, infantry, artillery, rushed pell-mell down the road leading back behind the forts of the city, only one of which, Mt. St. Quentin, had been able to play during the battle.

It was a grand mixing up of everything: officers riding about without men—men running down the hill without officers; fourgons had their wheels knocked off, caissons were upset, horses bruised, riders thrown—all intermingled with shouts, yells, and curses. The while wounded men were trying to keep up and crying for surgeons. Such a sight it rarely falls to the lot of man to witness.

The soldiers were throwing away their guns and side arms, in order to flee more rapidly; all seemed panic-stricken. The same was being enacted on other roads leading to Metz. I was in the midst of this, and now tore along at a mad pace—to stop would have been certain death.

It was some time before we reached the gates, notwithstanding the rapidity with which we got over the ground, and were nevertheless blocked before the Porte de France, which being very narrow but few could enter at a time.

So great was the stampede that it was only when we arrived at the Caserne du Génie that we saw that half the officers, men, and material of our ambulance corps were missing.

Mr. Good, surgeon-major, observed this, and in the absence of a higher officer, assumed command. I may here remark that Mr. Good had served for five years in the Southern army with Gen. Morgan, as surgeon-major; after which he came to Paris, and there graduated with the highest honor. He took service with the French at the outbreak of the war, and was recompensed for his gallantry by receiving the order of the Legion of Honor, in addition to the bronze cross afterward bestowed by the government upon all the officers of our ambulance corps. Dr. Good ordered us about, tired and hungry as we were. He stated that he believed the rest of the ambulance to be installed in some village not far distant, taking charge of wounded. We naturally experienced great trouble in getting started, and when we did start we went very slowly. Darkness was again upon us; the sky was overclouded, threatening to end the fair weather that had now lasted for several days. The troops were already taking up their quarters for the night by the roadside; and it was interesting to see the lights and shadows thrown upon them as they moved about the large camp-fires that were burning brightly. This was especially noticeable with the St. Germain dragoons, whose long red cloaks hung gracefully from their huge shoulders, while their plumes of the same color floated from their helmets. Coming to where the road made an acute angle with another, I perceived a brook just near. My horse was thirsty, and I stopped to let him drink. One of the fourgons followed my example. Upon looking up, we found the road again blocked up by a regiment of the line, through which it took us some time to make our way. I could find no trace of Mr. Good and his men, and thinking that they had perhaps had a chance to advance more rapidly, I rode on with the fourgon.

We had now reached another division of the road, and meeting a peasant, I asked him if he had seen anything of the rest of our ambulance. He said no; but that they must have taken the road we were upon, as he had seen several trains of cacolets coming from that direction. The road was at that moment comparatively free, and I improved the opportunity to move rapidly forward. Passing a rustic bridge over a valley stream, we were among our pickets, who were building fires and talking about the day's fighting.

It was necessary for me to stop for a few minutes in order to endeavor to gain some information, if possible, from them with reference to the missing portion of our ambulance. They could tell me nothing.

When I turned to go on, the fourgon was out of sight. I was entirely alone, and between the French and the Prussian lines. I proceeded at a lively canter, and had reached a portion of the road where on the one side is a wooded hill, on the other a brook. Just as I was on a level with the wood, bang! bang! bang! bang! went several shots, and I heard the balls whistle about me. I felt my cap raised. My horse staggered and fell. I laid down behind him as if dead, and quietly undid the bridle, cutting the saddle-girt with a large clasp-knife I always carried with me. These I slipped off.

The Prussians did not fire again, doubtless thinking me dead; but I could see dark forms moving about on the top of the hill against the murky sky.

I crept on my hands and knees down to the side of the brook, which fortunately had a row of bushes at its edge; behind these and in the water I slowly made my way back toward the French lines, holding my saddle and bridle up to keep them dry. I emerged from the brook just in time to meet a train of wounded coming from the direction of Châtel St. Germain. I asked them who occupied that hill, pointing back to the one from which the shots had come. One of them eyed me suspiciously, noticing that I was wet and had a saddle and bridle in my hand. I had joined them, and was walking along with them back to Metz.

"You are not a Frenchman," said another, to whom I

addressed some question upon the severity of the battle; "and we will have you arrested at the next village to see what you are."

To this I made no reply, but continued by the roadside.

Thanks to good fortune, I soon met Dr. Good and his men, who had come to a halt, and were inquiring about me.

In the marsh through which the road runs there, and only a few feet from it, were lying on the sward some five hundred French soldiers with a commandant. He told us that everything was upside down; that he had lost his regiment, and was going to pass the night there; moreover, that the woods all around were full of Prussians, whom, with true French enthusiasm, he expressed a desire to attack on his own account at daybreak.

He invited us to stay with him until then. This we declined to do. As we bade him good-night and drove off, he shouted after us, "You risk being shot at!" I was in one of the fourgons.

CHAPTER IX.

Dressing the Wounded in Châtel St. Germain—Neglect of an amputated Soldier—Lessy—I sleep in a Church surrounded by Dead—Arrest—Blind Man's Buff—The Prefecture and Jardin Fabert.

THIS I knew from what I had just experienced.

We drove over the very same road by the very same wood, determined to reach Châtel St. Germain, which we had been told was occupied by our troops. As we flew by the woods at a dead gallop, I saw my horse lying just where I had left him: the animal was not dead; for as one of our wheels passed over his leg, he gave a faint groan. Just then several more shots rang out, and the driver fell from his seat. Another of the men sprang to his place, and on we sped for life. Passing the wood, the road turned sharp to the right. In a few hundred yards we were again among French troops—on the outskirts of Châtel St. Germain, a village of the same character as the others in that department, the inhabitants being peasants, who, in accordance with the proclamation of Marshal Bazaine, had taken their effects, all their provisions, and entered Metz. Their deserted homes were occupied by troops and wounded. This fact accounts to some extent for the difficulty with which the siege of Metz, which now soon commenced, was carried on. As soon as their own provisions gave out, these peasants had to be nourished from the supplies of the town.

Ever since the commencement of the war, the roads leading to Metz from all directions were incumbered with families moving bed and baggage toward the city.

We drove into Châtel St. Germain. Almost the first building was the church, from whose steeple, dark as it was, we could see our flag flying, while before the door were stationed four of our fourgons.

On entering the church we found it full of wounded, bleeding and groaning: no straw had been scattered about, and they seemed to suffer intensely. None of these had been dressed, and had evidently been hours in that condition, as the clotted blood plainly showed. I took out my pocket instruments, a very handsome case, and proceeded to dress the wounds as fast as possible. The infirmiers brought me water from the baptismal font. Lint and bandages I always carried with me.

One of them with his huge foot stepped on my case of instruments, breaking many of the beautiful tortoise shell bistouris and other instruments. This was a great loss to me, and not easily repaired in those times.

After attending to these, I crossed the street and entered a house which was likewise filled with wounded, whom I proceeded to relieve. Most of them were on the first floor—the house being of wood and but one story high. The dead, dying, and wounded were huddled together in one large rooom with a door. I walked to this and opened it. Alone on the floor, in a small room, lay a man, whom I supposed from his position to be wounded; he was sitting half up leaning on his right hand; his head was sunken upon his breast. Going up to him I said, "Well, my man, where are you wounded?" He made no reply. I called for a lantern. The feeble light shone upon a face sad to behold. The man, a sergeant, was dead. His eyes, glaring from their sockets, were fixed intently upon the ground, while his lips were parted as if he were articulating a name. In his left hand he held something clutched tightly. I opened it and found a woman's portrait.

Among those in the large room were some quite severely wounded: one in particular whose case required an immediate amputation of the femur at the upper third. The muscles were crushed and torn, and the bone broken in two places—this was evidently the work of a shell. We were obliged to perform the operation with a bistouri, without chloroform, and it was very painful. Another had been already amputated at the humerus, lower third. The arteries had been taken up and tied, but no dressing of any kind had been given, and the strings hung from the raw flesh, the arm stump quivering in a nervous paroxysm.

We pass on to the next houses: all are full of wounded soldiers. We have hard work, and are assisted by some of the surgeons of the Guard. An adjutant of the staff comes to inform us that we must remove our wounded. To take all was impossible. We now began to convey them as fast as we could to the fourgons. It was hard to choose whom to take; of course we gave the more severely wounded the preference. When we went back into the church, from which we had taken several, for the last time, one poor fellow cried to us: "Do not leave me this way." But, alas! we could do nothing. All our wagons were filled, and all our men were on foot, every two carrying a wounded man on a stretcher. No horses or wagons were to be had in the village, and we were obliged to leave at least one hundred wounded to their fate. We sent the train containing one hundred and fifty wounded back to Metz. Dr. Lefort, M. Liégeois, Surgeon-Major Good, myself, and one under-assistant remained.

We now proceeded up the road in the direction of

Lessy, to see if we could obtain horses and wagons for the purpose of taking up the wounded left in Châtel St. Germain. There were but two horses and one rough wagon for drawing stones, in the place. These we pressed into service, and Surgeon-Major Good returned with myself. I drove, and a curious drive it was in the dark over the rugged country road. We had no stretchers or anything, save our pocket instruments; lint and bandages were all gone. We went back to the church and took eight, carrying them ourselves, and placing them in the wagon. While moving one, a hemorrhage came on, and we were obliged to make the ligature. I happened to have a box of wax-matches, which I lighted one after the other, while Good made the ligature. I gave him my handkerchief to bind about the wound, which was in the fore-arm just below the elbow, where the arteria brachialis is most superficial.

One of us had to drive the wagon back to Metz, a by-no-means agreeable undertaking. We drew lots. It fell to Good. Giving me his horse, he got up on the wagon, bade me good-night, and disappeared in the gloom.

I rode back to Lessy; but could find no traces of the others anywhere. I inquired at several houses without learning anything.

Observing a high wall with a little gothic portal, through which light was streaming, I rode thither, got off my horse, and leading him behind me, entered. The path led up through a churchyard to a chapel. About half-way up the path, and on a flat tomb, I saw a barrel from which wine was oozing; a tin cup and a candle were lying upon the ground beside it. There was no sign of any living being. As I was thirsty, I drank of the wine; and taking the light passed on to the chapel, whose walls were covered with moss and ivy. The door was open. It was midnight. I entered, taking the horse along with me.

A few French soldiers were lying upon the straw, which some one had scattered about for them. Upon examining them I found them all dead.

I tied my horse in the sacristy, and taking some straw from under the dead men, put it in one of the pews, where I laid down, and being worn out with the fatigue and exertion of the day, was soon asleep. Just near me, others were sleeping the sleep that knows no waking.

I was wakened by some one shaking me by the shoulder. Opening my eyes, I beheld two Prussian soldiers. "Français, prisonnier," they said. I got up, pointed to the band on my arm, and replied in German. They told me to follow. I went into the sacristy, untied the horse, and led him along. They saw that I was an officer, and behaved very well to me.

It seems that their troops had occupied the village at daybreak. I was taken before General V. Tümpling. He questioned me; and examining the little card that I carried with me, bearing the stamp of the provost marshal of the Army of the Rhine, he seemed satisfied.

Turning to his men, he ordered me blindfolded. What was going to happen next I did not know. There was a squad of soldiers just before the house where he had his headquarters. For a moment the thought flashed across my mind that I was going to be shot. I was soon re-assured, and the same two men led me off —one of them leading my horse, the other taking my arm.

How long that game of blind-man's buff lasted, I am unable to say: it seemed an age to me.

I was led through fields; made to climb fences, to

jump ditches, etc. At length, emerging from a small grove, I was halted in a lane.

Here the soldier turned me round this way and that some half dozen times. Then putting my face toward Metz, he said, "I will now undo your bandage. Mount your horse and ride back to your lines. We remain here; if you look back we fire upon you."

I obeyed; but as soon as I was out of range, looked about, but could see nothing in the shape of troops, except two horsemen on the top of a high hill: they were using a telescope.

Before me and not far distant were our lines, which I soon reached at a brisk gallop. Once more I was upon the main road.

August 19, 10 A. M. I reached a meadow just behind Fort St. Quentin. This fort was opening fire in the direction from which I had come. In the meadow I find half of my ambulance. In taking off my cap to salute, I see where the ball struck last night, leaving an ugly hole.

Dr. Good was there with the wagon. He told me that he endeavored to pass the lines about an hour ago in order to return it to its rightful owner. This he had found impossible, and we then attached it to our train. I got one of the horses and was soon on his back: he was a fine slick fellow, and I named him Lessy.

After a bite of cold bacon and bread, we retreated toward Metz, the fort still engaging with a Prussian battery. We encamped upon the side of a hill along with a regiment of artillery. The rain begins to fall, and mud soon forms. At 4 P. M. we return to the Caserne du Génie. This building was now filled up entirely, and we found in addition the large court occupied with trains of wounded for whom there was no place, and who were still lying in the wagons and on the stretchers, exposed to the inclemency of the weather.

Two of our surgeons, being of the number who had remained behind to take charge of the hospital, as I now term the barracks, came forward, and told us that they had sent to Marshal Bazaine in order to inform him of the state of things. The Marshal had at once sent an aid-de-camp to give us the Jardin Fabert and the Prefecture, out of which to make temporary hospitals. The Jardin Fabert is situated directly in front oft he Prefecture.

Thither we repaired, ordering the trains to follow. The inside of the Prefecture is palatial. Elegant paintings adorn the walls, while frescoes color the ceilings. Statuary, golden guéridons, etc., are to be seen on all sides; the smoothly polished floors bespeak luxury. The private apartments of the Emperor on the first floor were covered with the richest Turkey carpets. Magnificent oak sideboards adorned the dining salon below. A broad and beautiful flight of marble steps leads from the basement to the *bel etage*. Looking from the windows of the Prefecture we see the Jardin Fabert just across the highway that passes before it.

This garden, although so-called, was by no means what is understood by a garden in the general acceptation of the term. It consisted of hard ground; a lot, say, three hundred yards long by one hundred broad : on the river side was a low wall whose foot was washed by the Moselle; on the other was a sluice coming from a mill, so that we thus had water on three sides of us. This we considered a great advantage.

Our trains drew up in front of the Prefecture, and M. Lefort, Liégois, Good, and myself walked in, made an inspection, and soon set our men to work setting up beds and stretchers everywhere throughout the building— much to the disgust of several of Napoleon's lackeys who did not relish the attention we paid them, which was to order them, in the name of the Marshal Bazaine, commander-in-chief of the Army of the Rhine, to assist us. They could not refuse.

CHAPTER X.

The Emperor's Bed—Organization of our Ambulance and Régime for the Siege—Bazaine's First Sortie—Burning of Noiseville.

THE bloated lackeys, in their gilded tinsel, doing the drudgery of infirmiers, might have been an amusing sight to those who had time to study it.

We had the Prefecture soon filled up. A soldier of the line we placed in the very bed occupied by Napoleon himself only a few nights before.

Leaving Surgeon-Major Sauné, with four assistants, in charge of the Prefecture, we proceeded to make arrangements for the rest of the wounded, who were still in the wagons. We also filled a very large gymnastic hall, situated on the patch of ground known as the Jardin Fabert.

Our tents we next erected outside the building. These were likewise immediately filled. It was evening when our task was done. We were now divided into three divisions. Surgeons-Major Gilette and Martin, with four assistants and eight men each, had charge of the Caserne du Génie; Surgeon-Major Sauné, with four assistants and eight men, of the Prefecture; Surgeon-Major Good, with an equal number of assistants and men, of the Jardin Fabert.

That night we had no sleep, and were obliged to operate by such miserable light as we could get. I assisted at five amputations, four of which were of the upper extremity—three being of the humerus and one of the lower arm.

August 20. The Prussians have completely surrounded Metz. The French army, tired and exhausted from maneuvering and fighting, are encamped behind the forts. The city is blocked. Commencement of the siege.

We are now occupied in constructing a long wooden shed, that is to serve as a temporary hospital, in the Jardin Fabert. This takes some days, during which all is quiet on the lines.

August 28. We are regularly installed in the Jardin Fabert for the siege. All our eight tents up, besides several small additional ones. The gymnasium building, in which our Tuckers are put up, is full. Attached to this building, and opening into it by a door, is a small room, used in time of peace for holding the costumes of gymnasts. In this we store our medicine chests, instruments, lint, surgical appliances, etc. This we use as an operating room, a table having been procured from a café in the neighborhood. All our wounded in the caserne (I must here mention that there were two thousand in that building) were left to the regimental surgeons, who had assisted us in taking care of them. We contented ourselves with the Jardin Fabert and the Prefecture, which together contained three hundred wounded. Our ambulance, intended originally for three hundred wounded at the outside, had its hands full.

We are divided into wards. M. Liégeois, with two first-assistants, two under-assistants, and four men, takes one; each of the four surgeons-major, with two aids-major, two under-assistants, and four infirmiers, receive a ward also.

Over our camp floats the tricolor and the red cross. One corner of the garden is devoted to our smiths, while just opposite is the kitchen, and behind, a small tent for the infirmiers. In this they used to lounge, talk, and smoke when off duty.

Moreover, regular watches were appointed. At 7 in the morning, all the officers and men were to be present at roll-call, any absence being punishable by a deduction of one franc from the salary for officers, and fifty centimes for the men. Immediately after roll-call we had breakfast, and then went through the wards, giving the morning dressing, and performing operations, if any. At midday we dined in the "Black Eagle," a restaurant just across the river. At 2 in the afternoon we again visited the different services and gave the evening *pansement*. This ended the day.

At night, two officers, one assistant-major, one under-assistant, and one man for each service, were left in charge of the ambulance. The two officers slept in the little operating room. The four men were relieved at midnight. It was their duty to awake the officers and report anything that went wrong.

None of the men were allowed to go out of the ambulance at any time without a written order from the officers in charge.

The officers that slept in the little room went on duty at 6 in the evening, and were relieved at 6 the next evening—being, so to speak, officers of the day—and had the management of everything, subject to the approval of Dr. Lefort. This was our regular systematic programme, which we carried on all through the siege. In addition to the 300 wounded we now had under our supervision, we had also an out-service; that is, a service for wounded who were able to come every day from 9 to 12, and have their wounds dressed: two under-assistants, who were not otherwise employed, took charge of it.

August 29. The army has been quiet for a long time;

everything going on well. I ride through the camp in the direction of St. Quentin; the sunshine is magnificent. The camps present a gay and lively appearance. The different regimental bands practice every day. Soldiers are singing, dancing, and flirting with the cantinières. They seem in the best of spirits.

At 3 o'clock in the afternoon our infirmier, who was wounded at Gravelotte, died of peritonitis. This is an unusually long time for such wounded to linger; but his constitution had been a very strong one, and he was well cared for. Dr. Liégeois made the post-mortem. One hour later the body had been sewed up and consigned to its little wooden shell, over which we threw the tricolor. We now all stood in a circle about the coffin, while an appropriate address was made by the priest; in this he reminded us that our turn might come next.

We are on our way to the graveyard, behind the military hospital,—a slow and solemn procession, all on foot. We reach the fresh grave, and the remains of another of our little band sink to their last resting place. It is eventide.

August 30. The troops are maneuvering in the fields where they are encamped. The pyrotechnic institute of Metz, which has been manufacturing 30,000 cartridges a day, has supplied them with the ammunition of which they stood in need after the recent battles. They are ready for a brush, and every one looks forward to something to-morrow. Two deaths in our ambulance from pyæmia. We go through our duties as usual.

August 31. Pickets firing. At 3 P. M., a cannon-shot from the French, who have gone out beyond Fort St. Julien, east of Metz. After waiting a few minutes another, then another; as yet, no reply from the Prussians. The French column of attack being ordered forward, takes up the line of march in the direction of Noiseville, on the St. Avold and Strasbourg road. The Prussians open fire; an attack commences; the report of guns and musketry seem to be in the very streets of the town. Although our ambulance is full, yet half of us are ordered out. I am among them. We take four fourgons and ten stretchers; to each fourgon we harness four horses, and away we go at the grand gallop. Passing the Porte Allemande, we soon arrive on the field, and take our station in front of the Ferme de Bellecroix. This farm was at the angle of the Strasbourg road and the Chemin Creux. From here the country makes a slight depression: on this side were our troops, and on the other the Prussians; while the whole valley was one solid mass of smoke and flame. Fort St. Julien thundered its twenty-four pounders at the enemy. As the smoke rose a little, I could see a regiment charging in two lines, one man deep. They were mounting the opposite side, and already the first line was scaling the walls of St. Barbe. A detachment had just taken Noiseville, about two miles south of St. Barbe, and a little off the main road. No wounded came to us yet. Behind St. Barbe is a churchyard, in which, with the aid of my field-glass, I could clearly make out a body of Prussian troops. In an instant more I saw the French rise up on all sides, completely surrounding the churchyard. The Prussians thrust the butts of their muskets in the air, in sign of surrender. Our soldiers did not heed this, but shot them down without mercy. I could hear almost each report separately, observe the flash, and see the man fall. At dusk the fire relaxes. Reinforcements arrive. The French are victorious, and have advanced three miles—having first set fire to St. Barbe and Noiseville. The scenes in these villages are described by our soldiers as horrible—the dead bodies of old men and women lying in the burning streets. We descend the hill, and night coming on, we occupy a cottage, with a barn adjoining, leaving our horses in the stable and our wagons in the yard in front. This is the cottage of Lauvallières. All night long the rattle of musketry continues around us. A most peculiar effect is that caused by musket-firing at night, when one is at too great a distance to hear the reports—the flashes resemble lightning-bugs. This I could see far off. At 10 P. M., we lay down in the hay-mow, to pass a sleepless night.

September 1. At daylight we went to the cottage door and found it locked. Looking in the windows we saw it was deserted, and at once broke in the door. It was a low basement building. We made our way to the kitchen, where we found cups, coffee, black bread, etc. The floor was of stone. We built a large fire, around which we gathered to make coffee and drink it. The firing now commenced again, and with renewed vigor. This called us out. The rising sun found us standing in front of the barn conversing. A Prussian prisoner, wounded, was brought to us; he had a slight wound on his thumb. The wagons were gotten ready, and we proceeded up the hill, in the direction of the terrible cannonade that was going on. The shells, passing over our heads, fell beyond us. They were all percussion shells, and burst on striking any hard substance. We drove into Noiseville, which was still smoldering from last night's fire. This the French had taken at the point of the bayonet, and many dead Prussians were lying about everywhere. In a cellar, under guard, are 200 Prussian prisoners. The firing was now so terrific that the French were beginning to retreat; we moved with them. The 200 prisoners were ordered to fall in, two and two; they did so, and were now marched off under escort of a strong squad. Their muskets had been taken away from them when they were made prisoners. Their captain was at their head; his sword had likewise been taken from him. We all arrived together at the little inn where I had been on August 13th. In front of this, on a rude bench, sat Marshal Lebœuf. The morning was chilly, and he wore a huge military cloak, of dark-blue cloth. A few yards distant stood two of his staff, talking.

The Prussian prisoners were halted. The French officer, a lieutenant, commanding the squad placed over them, advanced, and held some conversation with Marshal Lebœuf. He returned, and told the Prussian officer and his men to come forward. The officer, with that pride so peculiar to a thoroughbred Prussian, saluted the Marshal, who said a few words to him; and then the whole party were sent off to Metz, to be imprisoned in one of the bastions. We entered the inn, on being informed by the Marshal himself, that there was a wounded Prussian on the first floor. We found him in one of the bedrooms: he had a severe wound in the abdomen. There was but little hope for him. He asked for water, and demanded to be taken to Metz. With both of these requests we complied. I aided M. Lefort to carry him down stairs and place him in one of our fourgons. We left the Inn de l' Ange, and, ascending the gentle elevation, were, in a few minutes, about fifty yards from the Ferme de Bellecroix. Here we halted. The road on either side was lined with heaps of finely broken stone. I got off my horse, tied him to a milepost, and sat down on one of these heaps to see the retreat. Immediately at my feet was the field, across which a general, with his staff, was galloping. The shells were literally raining about them. I saw one fall in their midst; dust and smoke followed, in which, for an instant, nothing was visible. When this cleared away two of their number were lying on the ground, while a third limped behind. Seeing our flag he came toward us. Men were running toward Bellecroix, and whenever they heard a shell coming they would throw themselves upon their faces and await the explosion. This is a good precaution, as well as a protection; for when a shell bursts the pieces fly up and out. I have seen men in this position escape entirely, and others who remained standing wounded from the same shell.

CHAPTER XI.

Asleep during Action—The Ambulance shelled—Progress of the Siege—Foraging Expedition.

BEING fatigued from watching the battle, I felt myself sinking, and was now reclining upon stones. I was soon fast asleep. I have no idea how long I remained there, but suddenly a shell came ringing and screaming only a few yards above my head. It passed over the road and fell in a field on the other side. I sprang up and found some men on their faces just near me, but the greater part were running as if the devil himself was after them. My horse was frightened, and gave a jerk at his halter. I went to him, untied, and mounted him. I was left entirely alone, all the rest having taken refuge in the farm of Bellecroix, whither I was not at that moment disposed to go, but rode out to the spot where the shell had exploded.

Here I dismounted, and digging for a few seconds in the dirt, succeeded in extracting a piece of it. I had not observed that a battery of mitrailleuse was coming up at full speed, and had barely time to get out of their way. They occupied this part of the hill, and got into position.

I turned to go back to Bellecroix. On the other side of the road was a battery of twelve-pounders, the guns pointed, the artillerymen at their places, only waiting the word "fire." As I rode into the yard at Bellecroix this battery commenced playing. We occupied the farm, where we found a part of the ambulance of the

Fourth Division. What they were doing there, when their main body was lying on the plain north of Metz, we did not think it our place to ask, but immediately set to work, in conjunction with them, to dress the wounded, who were coming in a few at a time. The wounded man on horseback, whom I had seen coming toward us some time back, proved to be General Manéque. A piece of shell had struck his horse in the shoulder-blade, and had likewise wounded him at the same time, fracturing the femur. It was impossible to enter into any treatment of this wound at that moment, and we sent the General back to Metz, where he had rooms in the Hotel de l'Europe.

We continued our duties. One of these men had a very peculiar wound. A ball putting out the right eye, had entered the socket and lodged in the fissura orbitalis superior. We had some difficulty in extracting it. The bone was not broken, but the point of the ball (which is of conical shape, somewhat similar to that used by the French), had evidently just had sufficient strength left to reach the fissure. We performed an excision of the eyeball. This case healed very quickly. Strange to say, the eyelids were untouched, and the patient was enabled thus to wear a glass eye. While we were performing the operation the patient fainted.

Having a few moments' leisure, I looked out of the window at the battle, that was still going on, but with less vigor. The French had now commenced a regular retreat. This, I must say, took place in good order—a great exception to the general rule. The infantry marched well, followed by the cavalry, riding side by side in a perfect column, although shells were falling among them as they retreated. The artillery covered. At 4 P. M. the firing ceased. We left Bellecroix and proceeded back toward Metz. When arrived about half-way to the city we turned off to a grove, distant only a few rods from the road. Here we halted and laid down under the trees. A breeze was springing up, and we took an hour's rest. When we awoke and started on, we saw the Imperial Guard passing by us in the direction of Borny. I asked one of them what was going on. He replied, winking good-humoredly, "Un mouvement stratégique." This is the expresssion the French always used when they were repulsed.

We got back to the Jardin Fabert at dusk, and had brought back no wounded with us, but had rendered a great deal of assistance on the field. This battle was very significant, in so far as it was Bazaine's first sortie, and had failed signally. We lost some fifteen hundred killed and wounded in this affair, the Prussians losing about one thousand men.

September 2. Everything goes on as usual. We learn that Marshal Bazaine's object in attacking yesterday was to move upon Thionville in case of success. The inhabitants of Metz, and the soldiers, do not yet seem to realize that we are really besieged, surrounded by a triple band of iron and fire, and cut off from all the world.

September 3. We attend to our duties as every day.

September 4. No change.

September 5. All quiet.

September 6. It is my turn to mount guard over the ambulance. I have an opportunity of observing how the different wards are kept. Am pestered for permission to go out by our infirmiers, and obliged to refuse many. At 10 P. M. I walk through all the wards, visiting each bed. One of the wounded in M. Liégeois' ward complains that they have forgotten to give him his two pills of opium. These I administer. I was surprised to find much neglect in this the ward of our surgeon-in-chief. One case in particular, a man whose gangrene was making slow progress from his feet upward. Yesterday morning it was confined to his foot alone, but now it had reached the inguinal region. The whole leg and thigh were green, and the man, still possessed of all his faculties, was in a state of living death. Other cases of carelessness I also noticed. From the whole tent issued a stench foul and strong. Having accomplished my inspection, I enter the little operating room. In this a bed had been erected for the officers on guard. I took off my coat and boots, and then pulling the blanket over me was soon forgetful of war and its chances.

September 7. A wet day. Roll-call at seven. During the morning visit I noticed that several officers were absent, having intrusted the dressing of their wounded to the infirmiers. The latter undertake this, handling the patient as if he were a log of wood. The unfortunate fellow cries out in pain, and grumbles at being left to such incompetent men. I hastened thither with my under-assistant, and soon relieved him. In the afternoon I also observe that the larger part of our officers are absent, and one whole ward received no dressing. I was obliged myself to perform this, and for the time forego my temporary supervision of the ambulance.

At 5 P. M. I wrote up my report, omitting nothing, and I was afterward informed that it was a dose for Dr. Lefort. The doctor expressed his approval, however, but I did not see much change in the future. Three of our wounded died during my guard, all of pyæmia.

September 8. The Intendance having made an inspection of the stores, now report to Marshal Bazaine. This report is concealed, but a proclamation is posted in all the streets, limiting the supply of bread to 400 grammes a day for adults; 200 grammes for children from four to twelve years; 100 grammes for those from one to four years. It was further announced that the supply of fresh meat was about to give out. All this looks rather blue, and people and soldiers alike begin to complain.

September 9. One death in our ambulance.

September 10. Our dead are taken to the city morgue, which is within the limits of the Jardin Fabert. We turn the morgue into a post-mortem room. Notwithstanding this, other bodies, those of civilians, are likewise sent. These we can not refuse, and it is very annoying.

September 11. Two operations: one resection of the hip-joint; one amputation of the femur.

September 12. There is an ambulance stationed up the river about half a mile above us, and we often see legs and arms floating down the stream, into which we also empty all our offal. This ambulance was called the "Ambulance of the Esplanade." The esplanade was a large garden and promenade on top of the city walls and in the embrasures. This was filled with rows of tents, in which the wounded were kept, to the number of seventeen hundred, under direction of the city civil authorities, who were always causing trouble with the military.

September 13. One death in our ambulance. These dead are all buried in the military graveyard.

September 14. Death of General Deceau, who, although wounded at the battle of Borny, and advised to leave the field, yet insisted upon remaining and directing the batteries under his command. Grand military funeral at 3 P. M. Deputations from all the army attended, while the general's whole division followed him to the grave, marching solemnly and with reversed muskets to the mournful strains of the dead march. The procession passes through the southern gate of Metz, and takes the route to the village of Plantières. Here the general is buried with all military honors, among others of his rank. Marshal Lebœuf read the funeral address, all the officers of his staff standing about the open grave. A fine rain is falling. There is no firing over the coffin, as in the American army. The soldiers file past, give one farewell look, and all is over.

September 19. The two who were operated on, on the 11th instant, die.

September 20. The rapidity with which our men die is perhaps striking, but statistics show that our losses daily average less than those of any other ambulance in the whole army.

I am on guard, and am called upon to sign the certificate of death for the first time, and am sorry to say that the responsibility was not considered a great one in those days; and whether the poor creatures were thrown into the grave half-alive or not, seemed to make but very little difference.

September 21. The siege begins to make itself keenly felt. There is no more hay for the horses.

September 22. A foraging expedition is made upon the barn of Lauvallières by a brigade of the Fourth Division, in the hope of finding fodder. They advance by stealth at 4 in the afternoon, and surround the barn, driving in the German pickets. They break open the door, and succeed in getting out some bundles of hay. This they throw hurriedly into wagons brought with them for that purpose. The Germans come up in time to prevent them from taking more. The French are driven back, but took with them what hay they could in the wagons, each soldier taking a bundle besides. During this I was in the Fort St. Julien, and could see all that was passing below me. I had gone up to "Infortuné's," a little restaurant just outside of the fort, and from which a good view of the surounding country to the north of Metz could be obtained. While at Infortuné's I could see in the valley a winding road. On this was a solitary house, from which a carriage drawn by two horses was hurrying in the direction of the enemy's lines. Presently I saw a very bright light, dazzling to look upon. This was evidently some signal, placed upon a high pole, and seemed at that distance to be made of a tin reflector, and turned toward the sun. While there sipping my coffee and conversing with some cavalry officers, my friend Montebello, a lieutenant of the guard, came in, carrying a sheep thrown across his shoulders. He was holding it by the legs, grasping two with each hand, and told me he had captured it. This was a great prize. At the commencement of the firing I had gone over to the fort. The sentinel refused me entrance at first. I then told him I knew Colonel Proetch. He saluted and allowed me to pass. The fort was still in progress of construction, and workmen were busy everywhere, digging trenches, building bastions, hauling stone, mounting guns, etc. In the center, and surrounded by the outworks, were the barracks. Passing by this, I entered the bastion where the firing was going on. It was a splendid battery of twenty-four pounders (brass, and planished off in the customary French style), commanding in the direction of Lauvallières, and covering our foragers' expedition. The colonel himself was directing the fire and aiming the guns. After each discharge he would spring up on the cavalier to follow the shell and see it strike, using his field-glass. He was just then firing at Servigny. Behind this village I could make out with the naked eye a regiment of Prussian cavalry. The shells of the colonel were well thrown, and presently I saw house after house struck, the shingles and plaster flying in all directions. It soon became too hot for the Prussians, who then darted off at full gallop into the woods behind. Col. Proetch had time to give them another shell. He had the satisfaction of seeing it burst in their midst. Several of them fell. This accomplished, he directed his fire upon a battery of the enemy, just opening fire a little further around to the south. This he soon silenced. Their shells all fell some hundred yards short of the fort, while the colonel's struck right in their battery. I now gave my attention to the brigade retreating from Lauvallières. The men here and there fell. Soon the firing ceased, and our soldiers fell back behind the trenches that they had thrown up. The hay they brought back with them did not last long, and we were soon again in a new dilemma.

On returning to the Jardin Fabert that evening, I was informed that a detachment from our ambulance had been on the field during the action of the day. They had dressed some fifty wounded, and brought back ten with them to Metz. These we found place for, some of our beds being vacant. A ball had entered the right leg of one of them, and passing through had entered the left leg, through which it likewise passed, and entered the leg of the man standing next to him, fracturing the femur, in which it remained. It is a curious fact, that the first man escaped without having any bones broken; while the other was obliged to be amputated, and died.

CHAPTER XII.

A Night with the Grand Guard—Privations—Death and Disease make Havoc among the Besieged—Metz "Sanitary Commission"—"Franc-Tireurs."

ON the following afternoon I was invited by Captain Charpelle, of the 12th regiment of the line, to visit him. He was to be on the grand guard that night, and asked me to stay with him until morning. I accepted; and having obtained permission to be absent until next roll-call, I started off in company with the captain, who having completed the little purchases he had come into Metz to make, declared himself at my disposal. We were both on foot. Captains in the French service are not mounted; those in the Prussian service, on the contrary, have horses assigned them by the government. We took the old St. Avold and Strasbourg route. How different now from what it was a month ago! All the beautiful trees had been cut down and split up for burning wood, as the cold weather sets in early in those parts, and no one knew how long the siege might continue. However, an army was every day expected to come from outside and raise the siege; in any case, both inhabitants and soldiers said they would never give up. I held some conversation with the captain as we walked along. He carried a cane cut from the bushes. This is a custom universally adopted by the French officers, and I have seen them in skirmishes directing their men and pointing with a cane. We now struck across the country, and passing under the walls of Fort St. Julien, came out at Infortuné's. From here the country made a steep declivity down to the edge of the Moselle, about five hundred yards distant. Down this was a railway, on which supplies were sent up from the river to the fort. Beside the railway was a narrow path; this we took. Gaining the bank of the river, we followed it for a short distance, and then turning up again, we arrived at the encampment of the 12th. The *diane* or evening bugle was sounding, and we sat down to some bread and a little bad brandy. There was not a cloud to be seen, and the stars were coming out one by one.

The grand guard is a body of men sent out beyond the ordinary pickets: this also sends out its pickets.

As soon as night had fairly come, he arose and said, "Let us go: it is time." It seems a battalion of his regiment, in which was his company, was already forward. We again neared the water's edge, and followed up the stream in the direction of Malroy, the first village occupied by the Germans. When we had gone about half a mile, we once more turned up and ascended the hill to a wood, in the edge of which were the last pickets. "Qui vive!" rang out upon the calm of the evening as a soldier brought his gun down to a charging position. This soldier was hidden in the brushes, from which he now sprang. "Douzième de la ligne," replied the captain. "Avance au mot." Charpelle advanced; gave the word, "Vivienne;" and we passed on. I saw soldiers stationed in squads here and there; others lying down in the wood, having prepared temporary huts from the boughs of trees for their officers. The night was advancing, and we laid down in the woods, both in the captain's sheep-skins. We talked for several hours. At 9 P. M. we could distinctly hear the Prussian bugles all along the line. Shortly after, all was quiet. Midnight struck in the village of Malroy: we could plainly count the strokes. The captain informed me that it was the hour for making his round, and asked me if I would like to go with him. I assented, and we started. The moon was high in the heavens, bathing the whole country with its beams, which fell like silver on the swift waters of the Moselle. We made our way over brushwood and stones, through a vineyard, in which the first squad was stationed. As we came up we were halted, and this time the mot d'ordre ("Vendôme") was called for and given. We passed on, and now climbed up the hill, catching hold of bushes and saplings to aid us in our ascent. On the top was a large field. On the edge of it nearest us was another squad. The moon shone full upon their dusky forms and bright weapons. The captain inquired if everything was going on right. The sergeant in command answered, "Yes." I can never forget the impression made upon me as two of these men came forward and aiming their muskets, which I knew were loaded, demanded the word from the captain. There was a sinister click in the locks. I felt that if by chance he had forgotten the word, we should be shot down like dogs. Before we left, the sergeant called our attention to some dark objects, bent over and running along the other side of the field. The captain ordered a volley fired at them. They disappeared, and all was still as death. Descending the hill, we visited another squad and then returned to our sheep-skins. The flash of the firing had evidently been seen by the Prussians in the valley, who now sent a shell or two into our woods, causing us to feel rather uneasy for a few minutes. They came whistling and screaming through the night, leaving a fiery wake behind them. We were not disturbed again until morning. At dawn we heard the Prussian réveille. In the French lines it is customary for the regimental bands to play immediately after the réveille; and the music, consisting of waltzes and Offenbach airs, now resounded for miles around. Below us and all about, the soldiers were lighting fires and making coffee. Since 1 A. M. a company of the sappers and miners have been cutting away at the wood in which we slept, from the other side, and now but few trees remain. After coffee, made in a large pan from which each one helped himself with a tin cup, the captain called in the pickets, and we all returned to camp together. Just as we were leaving, I saw the last trees that had given us shelter fall.

September 24. I came to the ambulance in time for roll-call. As I crossed by the same road we took yesterday, a battery of mitrailleuse is opening fire, while picket-firing is going on. We make the morning visit as usual. The siege is now well advanced, and our wants are increasing. Metz is literally filled to overflowing with the wounded. The "Sanitary Commission" are active in furnishing what means still remain in their power. Food it is impossible to give, and their gifts are restricted to clothing, blankets, boots, etc. The ladies of Metz make lint, and no old linen is wasted or sold to the Jew. Many of them visit the sick and wounded, bringing what little delicacies they still can. Most of the nurses in the Caserne du Génie were women. Some of these would come, from time to time, to our ambulance. We had a great deal of linen just then on hand, notwithstanding that everything else was beginning to fail. This we consigned to a little shed that we had erected for the purpose, outside of the gymnasium. We gave it to the charge of Madame Cohen and Madame Beton, two of the ladies of Metz who insisted upon rendering some service. The military hospital was full, and the municipal authorities offered the school-houses and one or two of the churches. These likewise were soon taken up. The demand for surgeons was very great, and by far exceeded the force. Notwithstanding that, we had the whole combined medical corps of the army (one thousand strong) with us. Many wounded were neglected, and died in consequence. All the civil doctors and medical students were pressed into the service, and still the work could not be accomplished. Metz was overloaded with wounded: forty thousand were within its narrow limits. Every day, death and disease made greater strides among them. The inhabitants offered their houses and took in a few wounded, but these were mostly officers and slightly wounded. The city presents the appearance of one vast hospital. Those who take wounded into their houses must have a card bearing the stamp of the Intendance subject to the approval of Dr. Lefort. A most surprising fact, and one that shows how badly everything was transacted (on the each-one-for-himself principle) is, that no one director had charge of the whole medical service of the army, nor had any one the supervision of the city department—each ambulance seemed to work for itself. The Intendance, it is true, professed to occupy themselves in a slight measure about it: but that they were not competent to the charge of their own department we had proof every day; and how could we expect them to enter into a branch of which they knew nothing. The use of our band, or brassard, on the left arm, became very general; and nurses, civilians, and every body else assumed it.

This may seem painted in rather disparaging colors; but having served in the French army will not blind me to faults. Such a state of confusion is seldom to be seen anywhere. It is all the more striking, as I supposed the

French army to be one of the finest and best-disciplined in Europe, when I entered it.

September 25. Five deaths in our ambulance. The typhoid fever is breaking out in the city. The fresh meat is all gone, and for three days past we have been eating horse flesh. A new proclamation is affixed to the walls, limiting the supply of bread to 300 grammes per diem for adults; the rations for children remain the same. A certain number of horses are detailed each day from the cavalry, to be slaughtered and eaten. All our meat at the restaurant is horse. One day we have horse-steaks; another, roast horse, etc. This does not agree with us, and many have cholera morbus. This afternoon the news of Sedan reaches us. The Prussians sent us in some French prisoners that they had taken there, in order that we might have the story from their own lips, the French refusing, as a rule, to believe any reports or statements coming from their enemies. The newspaper, the *Moniteur de la Moselle*, is printed daily. The supply of paper is giving out, and we now get the journal on a half-sheet of very inferior quality; generally on brown wrapping paper—sometimes on red paper, sometimes on blue, at others on yellow, then again on purple, etc. I have a batch of these papers before me, and consider them quite a curiosity. The news-venders brought us these papers every day, and were allowed to go, not only all through our lines, but also into the Prussian lines, so that the enemy knew exactly what was going on. In these papers was printed from day to day a detailed account of the French forces with the names of the generals commanding them, and the position they occupied. Moreover, an account of the remaining stores was given, and one editor advanced an opinion as to how long the siege would last.

September 26. Now commenced a rain. It pours down steadily; the river is rising.

October 1. The rain still continues; the Moselle is swollen and muddy, and the meadows are overflowed with water. Fort St. Quentin has been keeping up a steady fire for several days at the Prussians, who are building breastworks just beyond. The salt is giving out, and we have only enough left for a few days more. At supper, the Prussians answer Mont St. Quentin, and a brisk cannonade takes place. M. Liégeois cries out, in the midst of the talking and laughing, "Who wishes to go?" I volunteered; two out of the whole ambulance likewise came forward. We went upon the esplanade; the gutters were filled and water was running down the street leading to it. Still we went on. From the esplanade, where a large crowd of people had gathered to see the firing, we saw the shells flying back and forth. It was a beautiful sight! As they flashed from Mont St. Quentin it reminded me of a volcano. This firing lasted only a few minutes longer, and then all was still again, and no one went out.

October 2. My sleeping-quarters are now in the Hôtel de l'Europe, where are also several generals and lower officers. Mont St. Quentin again opens fire, and continues all day throwing projectiles into the enemy's camp. Of this they seem to take but little notice, replying only occasionally—sometimes not at all. The French are at their old tricks, wasting ammunition at a time when every ball or shell should tell. I have known a whole squad of them to fire at one man—and miss him. Their character is so excitable that they are easily overcome by a cool hand. Prussian officers have told me that when going into battle their men would be wounded or killed before they could get within a sufficient range to reach the French; but on coming, a large percentage of the balls went over their heads. This is attributed to the fact that the French in their flurry would forget to set the little *cran* on the barrel of the chassepôt marking the distance, right. And when they came nearer the enemy (supposing the *cran* to have been regulated 1,500 yards, and them now within 800 yards) the balls would go much too high, while the Prussians had only to pour in a fire underneath.

Skirmishing is going on every day. A corps of franc-tireurs is being organized at Metz. These are volunteers on their own responsibility, having officers who are in no way connected with the army, and correspond to our American guerilla. They scout and attack the enemy whenever they find an advantageous opportunity, and are constantly harassing them.

CHAPTER XIII.

Firing on the White Flag—The Garde Nationale—Grand Review—Interview with Marshal Bazaine—French Officers and Soldiers—Prussian Discipline.

THE uniform of this corps of franc-tireurs was gray, resembling that worn by the Confederate army, during the great rebellion in the United States. The franc-tireurs were, unfortunately, in equally bad odor both with French and Prussians. They spent their time, when off duty, in drinking and carousing; moreover, were generally seen in company with disreputable women. Their conduct aroused the indignation, not only of the whole army, which was bad enough itself, but also of the inhabitants. Marshal Bazaine sent word to warn them (they were 2,000 strong), that if such things continued, they should lay down their arms: to this they replied, by saying that "love and war went together."

October 3. The Prussians send a *parlementaire* into our lines. This takes place as follows: An officer speaking French, preceded by a trumpeter, and a soldier bearing the white flag, and followed by an orderly, rides forward; the flag having first been waved and the trumpet sounded. To this the French reply in like manner, and come forward to converse with the German. The Prussian parlementaire having gone through the preliminaries was now nearing our lines, when some of the franc-tireurs, who were concealed, lying behind stumps of trees, in brushwood, etc., fired upon him: he was missed; but his orderly being hit, fell from his horse. This ended the matter, and the Prussian turning, went back to his lines. It was never known who did this, beyond the fact that it was a franc-tireur. These latter endeavored to explain to the French authorities that it was all an accident.

About this time, in addition to the franc-tireurs, a National Guard is organized. This consists principally of shopkeepers and their clerks. Their uniform is brown, of the same shade as that worn by the regiment "Amis de France," in the Paris army. This regiment was composed entirely of strangers, and was hence also called "Le Regiment des Étrangers." In it were many of my compatriots. Dr. Good and myself were the only ones in the Army of the Rhine, although Mr. Eustis was in Metz during the whole siege—not from choice, however, as we shall presently see. The Americans and Swiss in the Paris army got but little thanks for their devotion to the cause of France; and when I returned to Paris, some months later, I saw one of them stopped in the street, accused of having been a spy, and barely escape being mobbed. This was after peace had been signed. I was also told by themselves, that others of their number had been subjected to like insults, and two had been arrested. Thanks to the kindness and energy of our minister, Mr. Washburne, who had remained at his post all during the siege of Paris, they were soon liberated.

The National Guard of Metz drill every day in front of the cathedral and in other public places. They blow their trumpets continually, and are a great nuisance. They number 3,000. They open recruiting offices. Here again we have another independent body of troops, recognizing no one but their own leaders. General Coffinières, commander of the garrison of Metz (consisting of regular soldiers) was on bad terms with the army encamped without the walls. This army was again a division of the armies of France, which, at the commencement of the war, numbered 300,000. This is the force that Napoleon was opposing the Germans with—whom he knew, and said, in his last proclamation, before leaving Paris, "had one of the best military organizations in Europe." They numbered over a million. The Garde Nationale at Metz soon began to assume authority, and did not hesitate to express their dislike to the rest of the army, but especially to Bazaine, who they said was a traitor, and would shoot, if he ever dared to think of handing their city over to the enemy. They were armed with old muzzle-loading muskets made over into breech-loaders, that now looked and worked something like the tabatière;—they had applied to the arsenal for chassepôts, which had been refused them. A most amusing feature is that they do not know the trumpet calls, and play the réveille at night, and the *diane* in the middle of the day; while they march to the music generally played to summon the soldiers to the distribution of rations, at 4 o'clock every afternoon—this, of course, is a very agreeable time, but rather out of place when a regiment is moving. This National Guard takes charge of the public buildings, turning off the regular soldiers who were stationed there.

October 4. Grand review of the National Guard, on the Place de la Cathédrale, to the amusement of everybody, including several of the soldiers of the line, whose eyes I could see twinkle laughingly as they watched these raw recruits go through the *manuel*. After exercising his troops for about half an hour, the colonel ordered them to form a hollow square about him: he then took from his pocket a scroll and read them an address, in which he said, among other things, that he alone could do nothing without the co-operation of the

Garde Nationale;—he trusted he should have this. [Cries of "Yes, yes!"] In conclusion, he called to their minds that they had to answer for the safety of Metz and of France. The review was then over, and the troops filed off, the band at their head playing very appropriately, "Voici le sabre, le sabre, le sabre de mon père;"—the ragamuffins of the town running after them and shouting, "hurrah." The whole affair caused much amusement.

It was a great mistake of allowing this National Guard to be formed. Just at that time, in other cities all over France, National Guards were also formed. When the war was over, and they were told to give up their arms, they refused: what the consequences were we saw under the Paris Commune, at Lyons, and Marseilles.

October 5. The rain has ceased, leaving us in mud, cold, and filth. Fort St. Quentin is still; there is no picket-firing. Everything and everybody looks neglected, and as if we could not hold out much longer. Soldiers and inhabitants appear careworn and weak. The bad nutriment is making fearful havoc on all sides. Dr. Lefort requests me to take a note to Marshal Bazaine, and see him in person. Mounting Lessy, I was soon outside the walls. Here a sad sight indeed presented itself to my view. The soldiers, half-starved, were moving languidly about their camps, which were literally sinks of mud; the water from the recent rain was still dripping from their little tents. These tents consist of four pieces of canvas and two small sticks two or three feet high. Every two soldiers carry a tent, each one having a half rolled up and strapped, with one of the sticks, on the top of his knapsack. The tent when put up is roof-shaped, and not of sufficient height to allow one to stand up, or even sit with comfort. Each tent is occupied by two soldiers.

As I rode through the muddy road, I could see several companies of cavalry, whose horses were already at the slaughter-house, on foot, and being taught the use of the chassepôt. Marshal Bazaine was residing in the village of Banc St. Martin, just off the large plain where so many soldiers were encamped. Turning to enter the road leading to his quarters, I saw the blue smoke rising from the fires at which they were drying their cloaks, drenched with rain. The house occupied by Marshal Bazaine was a very pretty one and by far the best in the village, being of wood, with a fine garden in front. Two sentinels were standing, one each side of the gate through which I rode. On entering, I saw two more sentinels at the porter's lodge. A squad of cavalry were standing about a fire in the yard. I dismounted, tied my horse, and went to the door of the villa, where two cavalrymen on foot, with drawn swords, halted me and asked my business. I told them, and was allowed to pass in. I was in a vestibule ornamented with stags' heads. Seeing a door open, I made my way to it and entered a large dining hall, in which several officers of the staff were sitting about a table drinking liquor. On seeing me, one of them arose, saluted, and asked my mission. He took the note, and saying he would be back in a minute, withdrew. He returned almost immediately and asked me please to follow him. He led me up a flight of steps to the first floor. Before a folding door on the landing stood two more sentinels. These saluted, and the officer, knocking, entered and announced Assistant Surgeon-Major Boyland, 1st Ambulance. The Marshal, who was sitting at a table writing, arose and offered me his hand. The room in which he was, occupied the southeast corner of the building, and commanded a view of all the camps on that side of Metz. It was plainly furnished in oak; a few engravings adorned the walls. Marshal Bazaine is a man about five feet five inches in height; rather corpulent; wore at that time a black moustache and imperial. He is slightly bald, and has gray hair. I handed him the note. He complimented me on my French patriotism, addressed me several questions about America, and then wrote. He was in fatigue uniform. "There," said he, "is your answer." Taking it, I arose, paid my respects, and withdrew.

This is the only time I ever saw Marshal Bazaine; indeed, he was hardly ever seen by any one outside of those immediately surrounding him. The officer, who had remained in the room all the time, accompanied me down stairs to the door, and there we parted. As I rode off at a brisk trot in the opposite direction from which I had approached, I observed a battery of mitrailleuse only a few yards from the villa, on the other side of the road. On my way back I saw several dead horses, which had evidently dropped down in the wet and dirt, and died from exhaustion. Men were also now beginning to die very fast, and almost every morning a few would be found dead in the tents from want of proper food and from cold. I returned to the ambulance and gave M. Lefort his answer.

October 6. One death in our ambulance. While in a barber's shop I met with an old acquaintance, Mr. Bishop, of London, who informed me that from motives of humanity he had come down to Metz while it was yet open, with an introduction to the abbess of the Convent of the Sacré Cœur, situated about two kilometres west of the city. He invites me to visit him there.

October 7. As the sun has now been shining for thirty-six hours and the roads are in a tolerable state of dryness, I saddle my horse and take the road to Montigny, that being the name of the village where the Sacré Cœur is situated. It is 4 o'clock in the afternoon. The houses just beyond the walls on this side seem to be in a better condition than those on the other side of Metz, some of which are entirely destroyed; others have nothing left but the bare frame, all around which lie shingles and plaster. These buildings were destroyed by the French troops, without any reason whatever, save, perhaps, that they were deserted, and their owners had gone in behind the city fortifications. These houses were behind the forts, and were not exposed to the enemy's fire. There seems to be no excuse for such unwarrantable destruction of private property. The only houses I saw entirely respected were the drinking-shops. I arrived in Montigny at 4½ P. M. This village consists of two long rows of buildings, one each side of the road. The best house seems to be the café, before which officers and soldiers are sitting together. This is one of the secrets of their indiscipline. The French officers, as a rule, have very little to boast of. The best of them are educated at St. Cyr, the course occupying three years, after which they think of decorations, wine, and women. Their habits and manners are very off-hand and easy, and they make free with the soldiers under them. These are ignorant; some can not read or write. Such cases came from time to time under my observation. The Prussian officers of the regular army require five years' hard study, after which they are stationed in some fortress or have charge of troops in province before they can take the field, all the time continuing their military education. The German soldiers can all read and write; some can speak French, and often a little English. When the scholars of a German gymnasium graduate, they are all required to make what is called the "abiturient" examination. They are then allowed to serve in the regular army for one year, instead of three, which they are obliged to serve if they do not pass this examination. Then they go to the reserve, to be called out in time of war. This system is an excellent one, and learns every man to be a soldier. It is in this way that the Landwehr is formed. Thus the Germans are always on a war-footing. Their Landsturm, embracing all men over forty-five and lads under eighteen, has been done away with, as it was found to be useless. The French soldiers, familiarized by their officers, become disrespectful and careless—a laxity of discipline being the natural consequence. I have never yet seen Prussian soldiers and officers sitting together in any public place: the officers hold themselves aloof from their men, whom they treat with the utmost severity; the men in their turn are taught, almost from their birth, to respect their officers. I have seen them sitting at a café in Berlin, and an officer came in. They got up, saluted, and remained standing until he passed them; they then immediately paid for what they had and left the café. Whenever they meet an officer anywhere, they salute. The French rarely salute any but the officers of their own regiment, and are dowdy and negligent in their dress, having none of that clean and trim appearance which always characterizes their enemies. I now turn down a narrow lane leading off the main road.

CHAPTER XIV.

Convent of the Sacré Cœur—The Convent Ambulance—Management of the Wards at Jardin Fabert.

High walls were on either side of this lane, above which, and a few rods on my right, I could see the Convent of the Sacré Cœur, with its castellated towers. It is an old stone building, situated in the midst of a vast park, at the other end of which flows the Moselle: a beautiful lawn slopes gradually from the front of the convent down to the water's edge. Behind was a finely laid out garden, which in summer must be charming. All through the park are long and wide avenues of elm-trees, from which the autumn leaves are falling. In the lane I pass several guns and gun-carriages, under the charge of a solitary artilleryman. I halt at a door in the convent wall. Upon ringing the bell a sister opens the little wicket, and peeps at me through it. "Mr. Bishop?" I inquire. Yes: would I please wait a minute? The sister hurried away, and soon came back. She opened the door to let me in. I told her I was afraid to leave my horse in the lane. She said she would go and tell the gardener to open the large gate just below. She soon returned; but Tholomyes, as she called him, was not there. So I rode in through the gate, that for the first time had been so desecrated. She showed me the gardener's house, and told me there was a stable in the rear. Thither I went, and tied my horse. I found Bishop sitting on one of the benches in the "Grande Avenue." We had some conversation together, after which he invited me to come up into the convent and be presented to the abbess. She was a charming lady, and gave me a little medal as a souvenir of the cloister, which, she said, was not often visited by gentlemen of the world. Taking leave of the abbess, we went into a long hall on the third story. This appeared to be a conversation-hall: chairs were set along in a row on one side. On the back of the chairs, which were of black leather (they were a present from the Empress), was the coat-of-arms of the imperial family of France, while old-fashioned portraits adorned the walls. The other side of the hall was taken up by long Gothic windows. Three small silver lamps were hanging from the ceiling. This hall occupied the whole length of the main building (to which there were two wings), and commanded a fine view of the country in front. Before one of the windows that was open was a huge telescope, working in all directions upon a high pedestal. Through this I obtained the best view of the Prussian outworks opposite Mont St. Quentin that I had during the entire siege of Metz. I could plainly see their guns, and the sentinels walking on the bastions. This outwork was on the top of a hill, was made of earth, and exactly square in form. Judging as well as the distance would allow me, the guns must have been of the largest size; this their reports when fired would go to confirm. On the hill side below this redoubt was a hamlet, between which and the former, soldiers in fatigue uniform were ascending and descending, carrying water, provisions, etc. In the village itself I could see Prussians moving about everywhere, their spiked helmets reflecting the sun brightly, and being distinctly visible. Presently a regiment left the hamlet and advanced a little way in our direction; they then disappeared in the thicket. Supper was served at 6. It was brought out to us under the trees in the park. We had tea and cow's meat. This latter was the greatest treat of the season, being the first fresh meat I had tasted for many a day. I enjoyed it thoroughly. After satisfying our appetites, Mr. Bishop proposed to me to walk through that part of the convent which was devoted to the wounded, and had hence received the name of "Ambulance du Sacré Cœur." The red cross floated over that wing of the building. We entered. On the first floor was a large waiting-room filled with wounded. There were twenty-four beds in this room. Everything appeared neat and clean,—the linen on the beds fresh, and the floor, which was of polished wood, scrupulously swept. The men looked well, in fact better than any I had seen in Metz. The windows were open at top, and there was sufficient ventilation. Several of the sisters had charge of this room. In a large closet adjoining were medicines, instruments, etc., and a good table. This ambulance is decidedly well managed, the position in the country being a great benefit to the wounded, who thus got purer air than those in the city. Ascending to the second story, there was another room and closet corresponding to those below—in the same orderly condition; on the third floor also. I inquired about surgical arrangements. It seems that the surgeon attached to the convent ordinarily had charge of this ambulance with his four assistants, the sisters taking the place of infirmiers. Having inspected the Ambulance of the Sacré Cœur, we descended the grand staircase, at the foot of which we were met by the surgeon himself, Dr. Mège. Mr. Bishop introduced me. Expressing my approval of everything connected with his ambulance, the doctor seemed pleased, and invited me into his studio, a fine suite of apartments on the ground floor. He told me that he made two visits a day—one in the morning, and one in the evening—in company with his assistants. He operated in the little apartments adjoining the large rooms; there also he was obliged to make his autopsies. He then showed me his reports of the last few days: out of seventy-two wounded, he had amputated four, only one of whom died. His wounded were now all doing well. Besides this, he told me that numerous out-patients came to his rooms daily from 10 to 12 o'clock. It was now 6.30 P. M., and knowing that during the siege the gates of the city closed at 7, I am loth to end an agreeable visit, and take my leave of the Sacré Cœur. Bishop accompanies me to the stable, and sees me off. Owing to some discrepancy in the clocks and watches, I reached Metz just in time to hear the chains clank, and see the drawbridge rise slowly from the moat. This settled the question. At a guard-house this side of the bridge was a company of chasseurs. I spoke to the officer in command: he seemed to think my being left outside a capital joke, and could do nothing for me. My only resource was to ride back to the convent. Fearing that perhaps this also closed its doors at 7, I clapped spurs to my horse, and hurried back to Montigny. Dashing down the little lane, I was again at the lodge. My worst expectations were realized, and I found myself locked out. As no one answered my first ring, I rang again; again no answer; after a third ring, however, I heard a flurry, as of women moving about and whispering. I waited in silence; at the expiration of nearly half an hour, the wicket was opened, and a sister holding up a candle, the better to see who the intruder might be, asked me what I wanted. She was not the one who had let me in that afternoon. I told her how I was situated, and that I wished to see Mr.

Bishop; she made no reply, but shut the wicket and disappeared. After waiting a few minutes more, I began to think that it was no use, and was just turning my horse with the intention of seeking a bed at the café, when there was an unbolting and unbarring of the large gateway. The gardener opened to me: he had a lantern in his hand, the light falling upon his gray head and bent form, while the old man leant upon a stick. Looking up at me, he said: "I have been here these fifty years, and never have known the like of this." I dismounted, gave him my horse, and walked along the veranda connecting the lodge with the building. In this I met several sisters hurrying by me in a very mysterious way; one stopped, and hung her head until I got past. By the pale light of the moon I could see that she was remarkably pretty, and there being no one near just at that moment, I lifted my cap, and was about to address her, when I saw Bishop coming. This ended the matter. The whole convent was now in a state of excitement seldom seen within its quiet walls. I could make out sisters passing before the windows with lights, while on the balcony in front of the main building stood Dr. Mège and the abbess. Bishop asked me what was up. I accompanied him to where the doctor and abbess were standing, and, with many apologies for my untimely visit, told them my story. They laughed heartily, and seemed very glad to see me back so soon. They conducted me to a reception-room, where, bidding me "good night," they left me with Bishop. On my arrival, the abbess had sent a sister to arrange me a room (next to Mr. Bishop's) which happened to be vacant. The sister now came and told me that it was ready, and Bishop and I started off to our quarters. After talking and smoking for an hour or so, we retired.

October 7. I am surprised, on awaking, to find myself in strange quarters. My adventure of last night explains it all. The best night's rest I have had since leaving Paris I had last night, and, I can now say, the best during the whole siege of Metz. Having taken a cup of coffee at the abbess' own table, I prepare to depart. She seemed to take great pleasure in teasing me about my confusion of last night. Bidding her adieu, and giving Bishop a shake of the hand, I am off. Galloping back, I arrive at the Jardin Fabert in time for roll-call, after which we make our visit. We find two dead in their beds in our ward—that is, Dr. Good's ward, whose first assistant I have the honor to be. After dressing the men all round, at 10 A. M., I am ordered out to superintend the dressing of the out-patients. This was carried on quite systematically. In the tent erected for this purpose were two long benches, one on each side; here the patients were made to sit down. On a table in the middle were all the requisite and necessary articles, such as water, alcohol, charpie, compresses, and bandages. The patients were dressed each in his turn. As soon as one was attended to, we sent him off, to make room for another. There were always two under-assistants employed here every morning: after finishing their wards, two first assistants would always come in and aid. The director paid a visit to this department regularly every morning. As many as one hundred wounded have been dressed here at one sitting; the least number at any one time during the siege being forty-five, our average being about seventy.

The management of the wards was as follows (as they were all managed alike, I take ours as a sample): We have one of the long tents directly behind the gymnasium building, which we can enter from that side by an outer door in the operating-room. This tent is a very high one, and really consists of two put together, having ventilators. It contained fifty beds—twenty-five on each side—leaving an aisle from one end to the other, while the beds are placed sufficiently far apart to leave room for the surgeon, assistants, and infirmiers. In the middle of the tent, but against its sides, so as to leave the passage clear, are two tables with racks and drawers, containing instruments and surgical appliances generally, including material for dressing wounds—oil, cloth, etc. On warm days the sides of the tent could be clewed up, thus allowing the air to circulate freely. Dr. Good was very strict in his duties, and the tent was well swept every morning before the visit. Our ward was one of the best, and the wounded fared well. The doctor went around from bed to bed every morning, attending to all the patients himself. In other words, each one of the first assistants received charge of twelve patients, being aided by one second assistant and four infirmiers, the surgeon-major at times operating himself, at others merely directing. While other surgeons in our ambulance were amputating and resecting whenever a good occasion offered itself, Dr. Good was strictly conservative, and, during the entire siege, only performed one operation,—this was an amputation of the humerus at the upper third, and was indispensably necessary. The ball had entered the arm, fracturing the bone at the point of insertion of the coraco-brachialis muscle, and made many splinters, which tore the other muscles, so that the whole arm from this region down was only hanging by the flesh. At dinner to-day he announced that his operation had been performed in the morning. It took place at 10 o'clock, in our tent. He objected to performing it in the little room generally designated for that purpose, owing to the fact that surgeons and assistants from the other wards were in the habit of crowding in when any operation was going on, as they used to do in the university clinics at Paris. We performed the operation at the bedside. I administered the chloroform; Lachapelle took up the arteries (in this he was assisted by MM. Ramelon and Brière); while the infirmiers passed sponges, water, etc. The doctor manifests the greatest possible *sang-froid* when operating; indeed, upon all occasions, his coolness is a subject of remark. He is a fine-looking man, six feet one and a half inches in height, thirty years of age, has chestnut-colored hair and mustaches, and piercing gray eyes. This amputation was performed quietly, neatly, and with rapidity: none of the other services knew anything about it until all was over. The circumstances were favorable. The patient had been brought in from a skirmish early that morning, having been wounded only a few hours previous. He was placed in a vacant bed in our tent at 9:30 A. M., and, as soon as the visit was over (we were just then making the last dressings), amputated.

CHAPTER XV.

Exposure of Wounds to the Air—Failing of Salt and Chloroform—The Consultation—Report of the Municipal Council—Skirmishing.

THIS patient, who was a young man of about twenty-eight years, soon got pyæmia, became delirious, and died. We were obliged to expose the wound more or less to the air. Exposure to the air causes suppuration, not so much from the contact of the wound with the air itself, as from the infectious matter the latter contains. Such is the case where the air is comparatively pure. No wonder that the pernicious influence was redoubled during the siege, when to breathe the air was almost sickening. There are some—for instance, Professor Billroth, of the Vienna University; and Professor Bardeleben, of Berlin—who assert that exposure to the air is beneficial to wounds in all stages, and prevents the formation of pus. This is contested by authorities equally distinguished: I may here name Sir William Fergusson, and Sir Henry Thompson, of London (the latter gentleman performed lithotrity on Napoleon at Chiselhurst).

As far as my own experience goes, the wounded that were kept in tents during the siege of Metz seemed to die more rapidly than those in the buildings: they did not linger so long, and the average rate of deaths was greater. Our ward was a particularly fortunate one. Whenever a fracture was brought us, we invariably applied the gutter and plaster bandage: first wrapping the limb in compresses soaked in oil, over which we put the plaster of Paris, leaving a *fenêtre* of sufficient size around the wound to allow cleansing and dressing. At every visit the wounds were first washed, and when deep, injected with one-third alcohol to two-thirds water, and the dressing changed regularly twice a day; medicines and aliments were given at precisely the same hour every day, and a strict régime carried out. Notwithstanding the fact that we lost less than any other ward in the 1st ambulance, our mortality was frightful; but this is to be attributed to causes which it was beyond our power to control. Everything was at this time beginning to fail. Our alcohol gone, we were obliged to have recourse to brandy and wine; but with these the infirmiers used to make free, and at last we saw ourselves reduced to cold water. This was taken from the Moselle, and was by no means clear or clean. At last our chloroform gave out, and we had to operate *à vif*, strapping the patient to the table and holding him down. In addition to all this, we had hospital gangrene. Things had reached such a pitch now, that the slightest wound became almost a matter of life and death. One case I have in mind, of a grenadier who had received a ball between the fourth and fifth metacarpal bones, neither of which had been broken—the ball had not even gone through the hand, and was easily extracted: this patient in four days was dead—pyæmia.

October 7 (continued). The weather is fine and the sun hot; a pestilential air prevails in and about the city; the dead who were buried in the different battle-fields are scarcely covered with earth. Dr. Lefort assured me that he had seen the toes and fingers of a half-buried man protruding from the ground in a field just in advance of Metz. The salt is now all gone; and we are obliged to eat the badly cooked horse-meat without.

The municipal council of Metz decided upon converting into salt, for culinary purposes, or at least into salt water, all the chlorhydric acid that could be procured. The distribution of this product, which was salt water, took place at the Mairie; first each ambulance receiving its supply, and then the rest of the army coming in for their share. This, in some degree, made up, but still did not give the same savor that salt itself would have done. One hundred and fifty litres were immediately delivered the soldiers, who, living upon bad bread and on horse-meat of inferior quality, are reduced to a sad extreme. Under these distressing circumstances, it is not remarkable that of the 60,000 wounded left us by the battles of Borny, Rezonville, Gravelotte, and Servigny, but 40,000 now remained. Our killed and missing had amounted to 20,000, making our total losses 80,000 men. The Prussians lost 70,000;—it is stated that on the 8th of August alone their losses were greater than during the whole war of 1866. The 40,000 are diminishing every day. A consultation is held by Dr. Lefort; M. Grellois, chief of the civil hospital of Metz; and Gen. Coffinières, —as to the best method of arranging the medical department. It was decided that five sections should be made; and the different ambulances were accordingly divided as follows:

1st Section.—Sixteen ambulances. Of these six were administered directly by the Intendance; five more were supported by them; five were carried on by the city authorities. *2d Section.*—Fifteen ambulances. Of these one was gratuitous; three carried on by the Intendance, and eleven by private citizens. *3d Section.*—Sixteen ambulances. Of these two were carried on gratuitously; three directly by the Intendance; five supported by them, and six by private citizens. *4th Section.*—Fourteen ambulances. Of these two were gratuitous; one directed by the Intendance; two supported by them; nine carried on by private citizens. *5th Section.*—Three ambulances: two supported by the Intendance, and one by private citizens.

In addition to this there was an ambulance established outside of the city walls, supported and directed by the Intendance. It was called "Le Polygone," being of polygonal shape. It consisted of long wooden sheds; the beds were on the floor, and only in a few wards were wooden frames erected. This ambulance was built on what used to be a large artillery park, and had by far the most wounded and sick (for typhus, typhoid, and diarrhea were making quick work) in or about Metz—in numbers 10,000. The deaths in the Polygone during the siege counted one thousand.

It will be seen from the above table that nearly all the ambulances were carried on or supported by the army Intendance and the inhabitants of Metz. The city authorities, although nominally directing but one ambulance, were by no means remiss in other ways, and gave, at the commencement of the siege, 294,142 francs to the "Sanitary Commission." (For the above statistics regarding sections, money, etc., I am indebted to the report of the municipal council of Metz, published in May, 1871.) Besides those just mentioned, was another ambulance, situated on the large vacant lot in front of the Caserne du Gènie, which is really a continuation of the esplanade. This consisted of four rows of freight cars (each row containing six) that had been pushed into the city, taken off the track, and drawn over the ground to the places assigned them. In these cars bunks were made, and each one resembled somewhat the forecastle of a ship. Steps were put up, and such arrangements made as the restricted circumstances would permit.

It was 4 o'clock in the afternoon before mentioned. Dr. Good and Surgeon-Major Sanné invite me to accompany them on a ride. I accept, and we all three start off a few minutes later. We take a narrow lane leading from the city up to Fort St. Julien: passing by this, and turning to our right we reached "La Ferme di Grimont," a small farm, with barns, poultry-yards, etc.; the latter, of course, has long since been emptied, nor was there any sign of dogs or cats (in Metz, also, I never saw a dog or cat after the first few days in October). The farm had been turned into a small fortress; trenches had been dug all around it; while in front a few field-pieces were stationed. The building consists of two towers, joined together by that which constitutes its main portion. The trees surrounding it had all been cut down, and scattered here and there. Wires had been drawn in different directions, so that if the enemy should, by any chance, arrive thus far, they would find themselves entangled, and give the French a good opportunity to pick them off. We rode up to the gate; it was locked, barred, and no one to be seen anywhere. Then we shouted; presently the sash of a window on the first floor was thrown up, and a head appeared: it was that of a general, who asked what we wanted. We replied that we were in search of Captain Charpille, whose regiment we knew had changed quarters.' The general then indicated the way we must take; and seeming not altogether pleased with the incident, drew in his head and banged down the window. It afterward turned out that this was General Gibon, commander of Charpille's division. Instead of following his directions, we descended the rugged road, crossed a stream running through the village of Merz, and were soon over at Bellecroix. There had been a great change here, the farm-house having been loopholed, and all the furniture—such as frames of looking-glasses, chairs, cradles, bedsteads, cupboards, etc.—broken up and used for fire-wood. About the farm had been made a deep moat. We remained here for some minutes, conversing with the officer in command, and watching the picket-firing, which was now commencing. From the Prussian side I could see some men shooting from behind trees; others from holes in the ground, their heads and shoulders only being visible. We left Bellecroix and took the main road back as far as its junction with the Borny route. Here we bore off to the right, and struck across a large field. In this several regiments were encamped: they had built two redoubts along their lines; and as we rode past the cannon's mouth, the soldiers came peering over the breastworks to see if we were friend or foe. Again we descended and passed through Merz. The picket-firing had now become quite brisk, taking the character of a skirmish. As we left Merz and rode on the other side, we met General Gibon. Turning in my saddle, and casting a glance behind me, I saw a regiment leave the redoubt, and march toward the enemy's lines. We turned into a vineyard at our right to watch them. Just then the Fort des Battes, on the Strasbourg road, opened fire to support them. To this a Prussian battery replied, and soon an engagement commenced. We could see this battery in a thicket about one thousand yards in front, from which the white smoke came with each discharge. I was conversing with Dr. Good: we looked up from the fire, and desiring to get onto higher ground, moved on. Sanné had disappeared. We took the road leading back to Grimont. As we passed under the walls of Fort St. Julien, the large siege guns commenced to play. It was splendid to hear their deep boom just above our heads, and then listen to the shells as they went whizzing through the air. We passed that side of the fort and came out on the Bouzonville route. This we followed for a few hundred yards, to where the last trenches were. On our right was a small redoubt: thither we went, and mounted the ramparts in order to get a better view of the fight that had now become quite serious. The reports of the musketry redouble; fresh troops are arriving. Just at our feet were some thirty or forty empty cacolets, in charge of infirmiers, awaiting the wounded. Suddenly a shell fell and exploded in their midst: one of the men was killed outright, and three more, also one mule, were wounded. This train now withdrew nearer the fort. We descended the ramparts and crossed the road into a patch of plowed ground, where we saw a battery, or at least part of a battery. The lieutenant in command had only two guns and six horses; not one man was with him. Immediately in front was the trench, from which one line was going out in open order, while another was coming up to take their places. We rode up to the lieutenant, who was a very young man, certainly not over twenty-one.

CHAPTER XVI.

In Front of Fort St. Julien—The Fight—A Shell explodes between Dr. Good and Myself—Struck by a Clod of Earth—Wounding of one of our Horses—Monitor Locomotives—Woippy.

THE shells and balls were now humming over our heads. As we approached the officer he saluted and seemed glad to get some one to talk to. He expressed his dissatisfaction at being left with his guns and horses entirely alone, in warm terms. Shells were at every moment falling and bursting near us. At every explosion this youthful lieutenant would put his hands to his ears, turn his back, and give a slight jump. Presently one fell not more than three feet in front of us—fortunately it did not explode, the ground being soft and the projectile having fallen on its side. He picked it up, saying: "If this had exploded we should not be alive now." We cautioned him about handling it. He said it was not dangerous now, and gave it a toss down the hill (it happened to be only a six-pounder). It struck and rolled; then about some thirty yards lower down, coming in contact with a stone, burst. No one was near. We spent a rather exciting hour there. From our position, which was, so to speak, a promontory, we could command a view of Metz and the surrounding country. On three sides of us volumes of smoke rose from bushes, woods, and plain, showing that the engagement had become general,—to which the roar of the cannon and the crackle of the musketry attested. We consulted a little pocket-map that I always carried with me, and found that we were not far from the village of Chieulles, in which was a Prussian post. To our left, and about half-way between us and this village, was one of the enemy's batteries. I could not help noticing it, as it was in a large open field: not a tree was anywhere near, nor had any works of defense been made; but they had simply galloped up, got into position, and commenced firing. This was not generally the case; for, from the different hills about Metz, the Prussians could see the least movement made in the French camps that lay at their feet. They had, moreover, thrown up breastworks: these they left oftentimes empty of guns, but always kept sentinels in them. When there was the least indication of an attack, these sentinels would signal the artillery, not far distant. In this way a comparatively small force would suffice; the French only attacking as a rule on one side—the fight of to-day being an exception. It was afterward ascertained that the Prussians had but 100,000 men around Metz; while the French, if we include the National Guard and the franc-tireurs, numbered nearly double that.

I looked at my watch, and saw that it was near 6 o'clock P. M.—the hour for evening rations. Dr. Good proposed that we should move on: at that very instant another shell came and burst before us. The officer went through his usual grimaces. The contract in the behavior of these two men struck me forcibly: the doctor, whose calm, composed nature never deserted him, did not move a muscle, although he knew, as we all did, that the next moment might be our last on earth. Good, turning to me, said, "Let us go and pick up a piece of that shell."

We bade the lieutenant good night, and proceeded to where the projectile had fallen. We halted: I got down and looked about for a piece of it, feeling that at any moment a second might come and land in the very same place (this happened very often). I soon found what I was looking for, and did not lose much time in picking it up and handing it to Dr. Good, in remembrance of our visit there. I had remounted, and we were but a few feet from this place, when there was a ring, a scream, and another shell fell exactly in the hole made by the first one. Hearing it coming, I leaned forward on my horse's neck, thinking that perhaps it would pass over me: almost at the same instant came the explosion, and I felt a severe blow in the middle of my back, and saw blood fly. Good's horse shied. "I am wounded in the back!" I cried. "No," said the doctor, who now rode up to brush me off with his hand, "it is only a clod of dirt." I felt like getting off my horse and saying a prayer of thanksgiving, but concluded to wait until out of range. I then told the doctor that I was sure I had seen blood fly; and he seeming to be all right, my eye fell upon his horse's croup. The mystery was explained: a piece of the missile had struck the poor animal, who was bleeding profusely, and tossing up his head as if suffering intensely. We could not stop to examine the wound then—not so much on account of the fire, that was falling off, as of the hour. We soon got safe behind Fort St. Julien, and descended the way that we had taken early in the afternoon. On either side of this were cavalry in camp, who had not been called out for this fight. Dr. Good, becoming anxious about his horse, who was losing blood quite fast, proposed that we should enter one of the camps and consult a veterinary surgeon. We found one standing on a small eminence at the farther end of the camp, and looking through his field-glasses up the valley in a northerly direction, where could be seen the red flashes from the Prussian outworks, which the evening made lurid. On the railroad track, which ran out to the limit of the French lines (Ladonchamps) unbroken, was a locomotive with iron sides built up on the principle of a monitor: these were loopholed; and the machine was made to dash out as far as possible, and pour volleys from each side into the enemy's ranks. The flames told us that the men inside were at work. That this system of railroad firing was impracticable, will be seen at a glance. In conversing subsequently with Gen. Blumenthal upon the subject, he said, "That is a very good plan if the enemy will stay along the railway." The locomotive in question was soon attacked by two batteries, and in a few seconds off went one or both (we could not see exactly at that distance) of the fore-wheels, and down came the machine on the track some distance from the French lines. There was no more firing from it. Upon asking the veterinary surgeon about Dr. Good's horse, he examined the wound and said that only the skin muscles and a few of the subcutaneous veins had been reached, and that the wound of itself had really but little significance. He washed and dressed it, and then invited us into his tent. This we declined, and wished him adieu with many thanks. As we were about to ride away, he said, " I am afraid for your horse, because he must be as badly fed as we are, and you know that even a scratch now-a-days may prove fatal." This was rather discouraging to Good, but turned out, alas! to be too true. The horse we were obliged to kill a few days after. The horses belonging to the Army of the Rhine were fast thinning out: those that did not go to the slaughter-house were exposed to cold, disease, and starvation. It was a pitiable sight to behold these wretched animals tied to stumps of trees or fence-rails. They had not been curried for some time, and their ribs literally protruded from their shaggy and mud-bespattered sides. They gave them dead leaves to eat in default of anything better.

The horses that stood privations and hardships the best were the Arabian horses. That is their characteristic. They are small and lazy, but can be made to travel very fast with a reasonable amount of whip and spur. They have to be tied some distance apart during the night—if not they will spend it in kicking and biting each other furiously. We had some 6,000 of these Arabians, brought from Algiers by the regiments of the African army—all stallions. One reason why this breed stood the siege so much better than the others is, that they are in the habit universally of eating their own manure, which, as their digestion is not very good, contains much that is nourishing. The six thousand were now reduced to twenty-eight hundred.

Dr. Good and myself returned to the Jardin Fabert, and giving our horses to the care of two infirmiers, went over to supper. To our surprise we found ourselves entirely alone. The waiter could not tell us where the others were. Having finished our repast we returned to the ambulance.

Just as we were entering, one of our wagons drove up, carrying six wounded. The second assistant in charge told me that at the commencement of the battle, all our effective had been ordered to the village of Woippy, north of Metz, and in the line of attack; moreover, that he had been ordered to deposit these wounded, and return for more. They were immediately placed in the empty beds, of which we had a fair supply. Saddling my horse, I prepared to go back with the fourgon. Dr.

Good remained behind with the officers and men on guard, in order to examine the fresh wounded. We started off, having first lighted a lantern, which we gave to the man sitting beside the driver. We had nothing to take with us, except a few provisions, such as wine, black bread, and raw horse-meat, for those who had had no supper; stretchers, lint bandages, etc., had been taken forward when the order came. We went as fast as our meager horses would allow us over the Thionville route. The firing was still going on, and had again become more lively. We passed several roadside inns, from the windows of which the light came streaming upon soldiers moving forward; while inside I could see others,—some were getting their wounds dressed, and a few were sitting at a table drinking. We had reached a barricade, and we were now obliged to turn to the left across a field, and enter Woippy from behind. The streets we found utterly deserted; the houses were vacant, and most of them closed. We halted about half way up the narrow street that we happened to be in, and seeing a light from one of the windows just near, I rode up, and drawing my revolver, knocked with the butt of it at a small door; all was still as the grave. The door was presently opened to me by Dr. Lefort himself. Attached to this house was a stable. Thither I went, having first ordered the men to take the bread and meat into the house. I dispatched the wagon under charge of Second-Assistant Brière to the other end of the village for wounded. When I went to Dr. Lefort he was sitting by a table in a large room, containing no other furniture than another chair and one long settee; the walls were perfectly bare, and moisture was upon them. A large fire-place completed the apartment, not forgetting two broken windows. The doctor was writing in a little memorandum-book. He told me that he was there waiting for the others, whom he had ordered to bring their wounded thither. "In the meantime," he said, "take two men; go out and inspect the village." Three of us started. I tried several doors of houses next this one, but they were locked. One of these I helped the men break in; on entering we found the house empty. On the floor of the cellar we found an old woman with her throat cut from ear to ear. Near by was a wine-cask empty. We conjectured that she had been murdered by some soldiers in order to get the wine.

Leaving this revolting scene, we crossed the street and went into the church. This was in good order, and the holy light was faintly burning above the altar. Its sole occupants were two dead captains. They were lying outside the chancel, and had evidently been brought there wounded. Two chairs had been thrown down, and they were leaning, half sitting up, against the backs of these. They seemed to have been left thus upon the cold stone floor. The resignation depicted in the face of one of them touched me; he had his hands folded in his lap, and the expression was soft and lifelike. He was an old man, and on his breast hung many a medal, doubtless well deserved. He had been wounded in the left temporal region, but was not in the least disfigured, although his weather-beaten and wrinkled forehead was blood-stained. Recrossing to the other side, I next visited a basement school-house. From this all the benches, chairs, desks, etc., had been taken; there was a plentiful supply of straw on the floor.

CHAPTER XVII.

Village of Woippy—Horrible Scenes—Charge of the Prussian Cavalry—The Wounded—Infernal Machines.

At one end of the low room was a huge black crucifix; lying upon the straw were a few wounded soldiers, to whom a Sister of Charity was giving water. None of them had been dressed. I took out my pocket case and visited them one after another. They were four in number. All had gunshot wounds. As we had no wagon or stretcher with us, these having all been sent forward, our only alternative was to carry them back to the house occupied by Dr. Lefort. First I sent one of my two men back to get another (two or three were loitering about the stable); we were thus four. We lifted the wounded men as carefully and gently as possible, making a chair or couch out of our eight hands. I did not trust them, two to each wounded soldier. Our task accomplished, we again set out, this time, however, for the other end of the village. In our way were many barricades, over which we were obliged to climb; and once I was precipitated into a deep ditch the other side of one. That was not all: the ditch was filled with water; and on endeavoring to scramble up the other side, which was slippery, I fell back a second time and sprained my ankle. This caused me some pain, and as the night was cold, my bath afforded me little comfort. However, I pressed forward as best I could, and now came to where the village stopped. The last house was an inn, called "Le Dragon." In front of this was a company of the

Imperial Guard. In the bar-room were some officers drinking and smoking. Opposite "The Dragon" was the post-office, also occupied by troops of the Guard. From this out, parallel with the road and very near it, a wide trench had been dug: the earth was thrown up on the north side, forming a high breastwork; so that when you walked upright your head was not exposed to the enemy's fire, which in this night attack was by no means slow. The trench extended for nearly half an English mile to another house with outbuildings, called the Maison Neuve, which we could make out when the flashes from the guns aided us. We could also see that in front of this farm considerable works of defense had been made, from which a battery of mitrailleuse was doing the work of death. We could further make out bodies of men, that we took to be officers, standing in the battery talking. These afterward proved to be some of our ambulance.

Seeing nothing of our wagons and infirmiers, I concluded to advance, and had already made some way when a colonel called out, "Get down into the trench, or you will be killed! We lost a captain, not half an hour ago, on the very spot you now occupy." This the whistle of bullets over my head seemed to attest. I took the colonel's advice, and ordered the men to follow me as I jumped down into the trench. We were moving rapidly in the direction of Maison Neuve. I could hear an officer say to his men, "Do not fire until you can almost touch them with the end of your bayonets, which use immediately after the discharge." The fire lulled for an instant. The bugle sounded. It was "Forward," and at the double-quick. Now the ammunition seemed to fail; and I heard an old soldier say to an officer, who had ordered him back to Woippy for fresh supplies, "In the old days of the Crimea we used to send our ammunition hours in advance." It was very unfortunate for the French that cartridges should be wanting at this moment, as they were in the midst of a closely contested fight: still it could not be helped then; and back the soldier went to order the cartridges forward. He was on foot. Whether he ever reached the village or not I never knew, for he had been absent but a few minutes when the thunder of a Prussian cavalry regiment reached our ears. On they came, swift as the wind and shouting fiercely. They were charging the trench. Our soldiers rose up, and having a few more rounds left, poured several volleys into them, while the battery gave them a broadside. It was frightful to see them falling, which the light caused by the battery enabled us to do so. They were unable to arrive, and the few that remained turned back. Three only, who tempted death, dashed up and mounted the outwork. They were riddled with bullets; and one (horse and rider) that had reached the top fell over into the trench, crushing to death a soldier standing but a few feet from me, and to whom I had just been talking. The rumble caused as this heavy mass rolled suddenly down the embankment somewhat startled me. I examined the man, to see if any life was left in him. His whole side was torn open, stomach and heart protruding, while the skull was fractured in several places and the legs well shot. The horse had come off no better. We climbed over this mass of bleeding flesh, and went on in the direction of the farm.

On arriving in the battery, M. Liégeois came forward, and expressed great surprise when I told him what had happened. The firing was fast ceasing; and I had been there but a few minutes, when all was still.

We turned and went into a yard which was just behind the farm-house. It was of quadrangular shape, formed by the buildings, four in number, and was filled with cacolets, charettes, and our wagons, between which it was extremely difficult to make our way. We had entered through a gate that formed one angle of this inclosure. The first edifice on our right was the dwelling. It was then occupied by a regimental surgeon, Dr. Deblé, of the 7th Guards, who had established his field ambulance there. The doctor was performing an amputation as I walked in: this I was surprised at, being the first time I had ever seen such prompt action in any ambulance belonging to the French army. Those who were not engaged at the operation were dressing wounds and carrying those that had already been cared for, to the charettes and cacolets. The barns had also been similarly taken possession of. In one of these, a portion of our medical corps were installed. On stretchers placed in rows on the floor lay the wounded. Surgeons-Major Sanné and Gillette, supported by their 1st and 2d assistants, were hard at work. Already thirteen of this lot (they counted twenty-six in all) had received a first dressing. I told M. Liégeois that Dr. Lefort was expecting them back at Woippy, but he replied that the wounded could be attended to better where they were, and then sent to Metz. The other thirteen we got ready as soon as possible, and transported them from the barn to our wagons. Before the men drove off, we gave them orders to deposit the wounded and return, as a renewal of the battle was expected at daylight. The train left, taking with them everything; the only traces of our visit were blood-stains on the floor. They took a different route, while we returned to Woippy along the road. The stars were shining brightly, but there was no moon. As we passed along we could see the dark forms of the dead lying in the trenches, of which they were now the only occupants.

It was near 11 p. m. when we returned to the house in which we had left Dr. Lefort, to whom we reported at once all that had taken place. He expressed his satisfaction, and invited us all to sit down. We drew around the wide, old-fashioned table. The chill air of the night came through the broken panes. There was no wood for fuel, and we did not know what to do to get warm. I told the doctor that if he would give me four men I would in fifteen minutes bring wood enough for a roaring fire. He assented, and taking the four infirmiers I went first to the stable, where I found an ax and a crowbar. Signing one of the men to carry this, while I shouldered the ax, we repaired at once to the church, and then commenced a banging, smashing, and crashing. We were breaking down the pews. This made a horrid noise, the dead captains still lying before the chancel. When we had a sufficient quantity of wood, we split it up, and each taking an armful returned to our fireside. Our companions cheered us as they saw the fuel, and we soon built a splendid fire. We made one more visit to the church, and this time brought back enough to last us until morning. This may seem a desecration of the sanctuary; but such is war. Wine and bread were brought out, and we all fell to with a good relish. Most of our officers and men had eaten nothing since dinner. The bread we were now eating was black and heavy, made out of oatmeal. In it we often found small pebbles, sand, straw, oats, etc. It was exceedingly unhealthy, and the cause of much diarrhea and typhoid fever. Between a risk of these and certain starvation we had to choose. This miserable and scant nourishment has, besides the effect on the general system, a direct bad influence on the liver. It will be readily understood that all were weak and dejected. To make matters worse, there seemed to be no help for us now. We did not know how long the siege might continue, and began to despair. After eating, we sat talking, smoking, and looking into the embers. The fire was burning low, and being tired, I dropped off to sleep. When I awoke the fire was burning brightly again and daylight was coming through the window. The other officers, who had slept on the floor, were getting up, while the men were coming in from the stable, which they had occupied during the night. All our wagons and material were now arrived, and we set three of our infirmiers to work at warming wine, after which orders were given to hold ourselves in readiness for action. I passed out into the cool morning air, and entered the large field which lies between Woippy and the walls of Metz. The sky was clouded, but gilded by the first rays of the rising sun. The bugles rang about me on all sides, and everywhere I heard beautiful music. In a few minutes I returned. Dr. Lefort then ordered myself and M. Mullet, a medical commissary, forward to reconnoiter the scene of the action of yesterday. Picket-firing was going on as we rode around the village, barricades making a detour necessary. We next struck into the same road we had taken last night, and a short gallop brought us to Maison Rouge. The surrounding country presented a different aspect from when we had last seen it. Running from the trench that we had been in last night was another of about equal length, the two meeting and forming a right angle. Behind a great mound immediately in front of the farm, stood a general and several officers of the staff, conversing. As we came up, they halted us and objected to our passing. We explained to them that we wished to go out to Ladonchamps, a château situated a short distance in advance, which was occupied by the first line; between this and Maison Neuve, the second line, a communication had been established by the last-mentioned trench. We gave the word (Châlons), told them that we were after wounded, and went on. We had some difficulty in picking our way out through the sharp spikes the French had driven down. They had also put up *chevaux-de-frise*, which is nothing more than a wooden work resembling an ordinary harrow turned on end, but more especially the frames, which are used to kill calves on in the country. Moreover, they had dug pits here and there, and in fact made all sorts of infernal arrangements, including broken glass, which was scattered everywhere about, and which we barely escaped getting into our horses' feet. At length we got through and reached the level road. We then struck into a brisk trot, and did not slacken until we had reached Ladonchamps. Here were other trenches, right and left, but connecting together. All were filled with soldiers.

CHAPTER XVIII.

The Trenches—Napoleon's Portrait by a Prussian Artist—St. Agathe—
The Tobacco Factory turned into an Ambulance — Fate of the
Wounded—Marshal Bazaine.

THESE were chasseurs of the Guard, leaning forward, aiming their chassepôts, and firing at random, to which the enemy replied but feebly. In front of the building, and across the road, ran a barricade, of which a company of lancers, on foot, were taking charge. The château of Ladonchamps was a large and handsome edifice, built after the style of architecture existing during the reign of Louis XIV, with four towers and a large court. It was exactly square in shape. In this was included barns, etc., there being no other out-houses. This château had been the point of combat on several occasions, having been taken by the Prussians and retaken by the French, in whose hands it remained until Metz fell. The roof was broken in very many places where the shells had struck; the walls were riddled with bullet-holes. The court into which we now rode contained pieces of projectiles of different size and character, that had evidently gone over the buildings and fallen within. The windows were all in pieces. We went first to the stable, in which we found a few dead soldiers. We dismounted, tied our horses, then crossing the court, went up a flight of white marble steps, and crawled through a panel in the broken door into a large room, that we took to be the former dining-hall. There was not a vestige of anything save a few empty bottles labeled "Cognac," and a cracked glass. On the wall, where were still left a few traces of frescoe, was a rude sketch of Napoleon absconding: this represented him in the costume worn by his uncle (the famous gray coat and chapeau). He had a small bundle done up in a handkerchief, through which his stick was poked and flung across his shoulder. He was in the act of jumping a brook; a small dog was barking at him, while behind could be seen a Prussian soldier in pursuit, his bayonet being very close to Napoleon's back. Underneath was written, in German, "*Hoch lebe Napoleon.*" The whole thing was done in charcoal, by the Prussians, while they were there. We went up to the first floor, where we found some old sabers, muskets, and helmets. Coming down, we again remounted, and went out into a small grove behind: this was occupied by artillery. Looking north, we could plainly see the enemy, only a few hundred yards distant. They were at an inn called "Grande Étape." Some were standing in front, others were in trenches. We asked one of the artillerymen if there were any wounded in that direction. "Oh, yes!" he said. "I have just come from St. Agathe, where there are many." St. Agathe was an ordinary farm, about one thousand yards west of Ladonchamps. Upon learning this from the soldier, I asked for the regimental surgeon, and consulted him. He confirmed the statement, and we forthwith put spurs to our steeds and regained the village of Woippy. The picket-firing had ceased. As soon as we had reported to Dr. Lefort, he ordered the whole train forward. Everything was ready, and we started at once.

We were already crossing the meadow lying between Woippy and St. Agathe. In front walked three infirmiers, one of whom carried the Red Cross, on white ground, which hung mournfully in the still morning air. We reached St. Agathe withot delay. It was a long, low house (basement), and had been the dwelling of peasants. A battalion occupied it. The muddy yard was strewn with bits of wood, old képis, and arms. The barn had been devoted to the wounded. Before this our train halted. On the floor, without straw, stretcher, or anything else, were half-a-dozen wounded men. We wanted to dress them before moving, and had already commenced, when the commandant requested us to defer it until we should have a more convenient opportunity, saying that he wished to commence firing. We remonstrated, but in vain, and were obliged to carry the wounded men to the wagons. Five only we took—the sixth was so far gone that it was useless to disturb him; his liver and all his intestines were torn open, and life still lingered. We took him for a German at first, as he wore a Prussian overcoat. This had, doubtless, been taken from one of the enemy that he had killed. It was a universal custom in those days, when a man was shot, to run out and rob him, even at the risk of life. The first thing looked after was newspapers; and most of our news from outside was obtained in this way. We left this man to his fate. A fine rain now began to fall. We left the Ferme of St. Agathe. The burly commandant, with his fierce mustaches and a revolver stuck in his girdle, seemed glad to get rid of us. In a few seconds the sharp crack of rifles told us that he had commenced operations. Arriving at Maison Neuve, we did not go back to Woippy, but proceeded at once toward Metz, by the route which our wagons had taken last night. The road was clear, and we moved quickly over it. Entering by the Porte de France, we soon reached the Jardin Fabert. Out of the twenty-five sent last night we had only been able to receive five;

the other twenty we sent to the railroad cars, in front of the Caserne du Génie. We also sent the five that we now had with us thither. They came back in half an hour, and the director of that ambulance, M. Jacquin, sent word that all places were now full. We lost some little time in deciding what we should do with this lot. We gave them an examination and dressing while they were still lying in the wagons in front of our ambulance. The rain had increased, and came down heavily. In the meantime a messenger had been dispatched to Marshal Bazaine, who at once replied by assigning us the large tobacco fabrique of Metz. Thither we at once repaired, and deposited our wounded. It was a building of immense length, and four stories high. Here we established a branch ambulance, and hoisted our flag. The room in which we placed our wounded extended the whole length of one side, and was on the ground floor. Piles of tobacco leaf lined the walls, leaving a great wide space between them, in which we placed our wounded: we had no beds, and left them the stretchers on which they had been brought. One of them we were obliged to amputate. After sending an infirmier for the instruments we laid the patient on one of the piles of tobacco leaves—we had no table. Eight of our men held him down while we performed the operation. This looked more like butchery than anything I had yet seen. The femoral artery was compressed by myself. We had to use the compression by hand. Many authors have contested this, advancing arguments in favor of the tourniquet. The compression by hand has a double advantage: the hand can be changed, and, when great force is necessary, both applied, one over the other, so as to allow a change of position if the assistant becomes tired, which often happens during a long operation. That the tourniquet, as made by Dupuytren, and improved upon by Pardoleben, has undoubted advantages in certain cases is undeniable. We had no tourniquet among our apparatus, which was supposed to be very complete; but we did have a complete set of obstetrical instruments. This fact caused much amusement. Said instruments had never been opened since we left Paris. This patient died a few days after the operation, of *infection purulente*. The amputation, as all our others, as far as possible had been made with two laps. The circular method was only once put into practice. We visited this branch of our medical department regularly, twice a day, immediately after performing our duties at the Jardin Fabert. I noticed that these wounded, at first, seemed to do better than the others; but soon they began to fall off. One died, then another, and but two were now left; and these were in so bad a condition that we could not think of moving them. Doubtless the tobacco, with which the room and whole building was impregnated, acted as a narcotic, and thus aided in producing pyæmia.

Among the other diseases pervading the Army of the Rhine there was a great deal of palpitation of the heart. This was almost entirely confined to those who were able to go about. To this, however, all soldiers exposed to great fatigue, long marches, etc., are liable—not so much on account of the exertion, as by reason of their being loaded down with accoutrements. A knapsack pressing for hours here, a strap there, etc., naturally prevents the circulation of the blood about those places—if not entirely, at least in part. This causes a greater action of the heart, and produces palpitation.

Thus ended our branch ambulance; and this battle being the last before the capitulation, we received no more wounded.

The affair of Ladonchamps was looked upon by all as Marshal Bazaine's final effort to break through the Prussian lines. Several days before, different indications announced a movement, and all looked forward, with, it is true, faint hope, to the raising of the siege and the departure of the army. The soldiers had received a week's rations, and the army train had been half reorganized. The number of wagons was necessarily reduced, on account of the want of horses. Besides, a grand council of war had been held at headquarters, which was attended by all the generals commanding army corps, in addition to the principal heads of the different departments. It was known later, however, that only secondary matters were discussed. The rumor of departure was more and more believed in. To this supposition the order issued to send all men who were not perfectly valid into the ambulances, and other measures, gave more weight. That a movement in the plain of Thionville would take place, was in everybody's mouth four days before it actually occurred. Metz was known to contain many spies; and the Prussians, always well informed of what the French were doing, took their precautions accordingly— with what success we have seen. This attack received the name of a foraging expedition. I now translate a few lines from the French official report, on that day's transactions: "In presence of the intensity of the enemy's fire, which did not diminish throughout the battle, and was concentrated upon us from all points, it was not possible to carry out the foraging movement as I expected. Our wagons could not cross the plowed ground under such a storm of ball and shell, and I was obliged to make them return to their camps. I let them remain in the field some time, *afin d'affirmer nos succès* (to show that we had won), and did not give the order until half past 5 o'clock, to fall within our lines. The retreat took place in the best order, under protection of our field artillery and batteries in position." The French, although badly whipped again, would not acknowledge it. Marshal Bazaine's report continues: "Although the projected foraging expedition was unable to take place, this day constitutes none the less, for our arms, *un brilliant succès*. Our soldiers behaved with the utmost valor, and chased the enemy from all their positions. They abandoned their trenches and fled in confusion. Unfortunately our losses were serious— 1,257 put *hors de combat*, as follows: Officers killed, 11; wounded, 53; among whom are three staff-officers. Troops: 90 killed, 981 wounded, 122 missing. Those of the enemy (Third Corps, and General von Kümmer's division) were 65 officers and 1,665 men, without counting the 535 prisoners that we took. These prisoners were mostly Poles, from the grand duchy of Posen, belonging to the 68th and 69th regiments of Prussian infantry, who surrendered without combat, and came forward to kiss the hands of the Abbé Laucier, who was present on the field of battle."

This report was all very fine, but was greatly exaggerated, as far as numbers were concerned: then again, where the Marshal saw a brilliant success, must have been "in his mind's eye."

CHAPTER XIX.

The Polish Prisoners—Prussian Rations—Proclamation with Reference to Flour and Wheat—The Hotel de Ville—Demonstration by the National Guard—Cries against Bazaine.

It is true that we took some prisoners, and that these were mostly Poles belonging to the Prussian Landwehr. The Poles bear but little sympathy or friendship toward the Prussians, as they are forced to serve in that army, whether they will or not: consequently they used every opportunity to desert to the French, knowing that they would be well treated by them. Under the Second Empire a pension was allowed to all Poles living in France who could find no means of employment. Among the few wounded that we received after Ladonchamps, were three of these unfortunates: they seemed very downhearted and homesick; often speaking of their wives, their children, and the little fireside far away. Two of them died. The survivor, who was a Jew, said he was afraid he should be shot as a deserter when the Prussians came into Metz; but we assured him that we could testify to the fact that he had been taken prisoner, for which his wound was also a guaranty. With this latter, which was only an abrasion of the skin, he seemed very well satisfied, informing us that he would now get a pension from his government, and thus be enabled to enlarge his store when he got back home. We questioned him about rations in the Prussian army, as he always used to turn up his nose at the food we gave, which was the best we had. He said that he and every one got coffee and bread in the morning; *"erbst wurst*," with boiled beef and potatoes at noon; "*erbst wurst*" and a pound of pork at night;—moreover, brandy and cigars—supplies of which were continually sent down from the rear. This "*erbst wurst*," or vegetable sausage, is like a bologna sausage in form, of a light yellow color, enveloped in tin-foil, and is easily carried in the knapsack. If you cut off a piece—say four inches long, and throw it into a caldron of hot water, in a very few minutes you have a heavy and rich vegetable soup containing small pieces of meat. This sausage is to be submitted to the Paris Medical Academy, who will doubtless adopt it in the French army.

October 9. The rain continues; cold gusts of wind whistle over the camps; the poor soldiers, standing in the muddy trenches, endeavor to shield themselves from the storm that drives through them. Four deaths in our ambulance. Everybody looks emaciated and care-worn. Our sugar has been gone for some time, and we have only coffee for a few days more. Mont St. Quentin and St. Julien are firing heavily; our position is horrible. The inhabitants of Metz distressed, and many of them sick, appeal to the army: a subscription is made among the officers amounting to 50,000 francs; but, alas! what could one do with money, when thousands could not purchase fresh food? The situation of the city and the army is becoming every day more critical as regards aliments. The following proclamation appears:

"All those having any wheat or flour concealed, are hereby ordered to declare the same at the *Mairie* of Metz before Tuesday, the 11th October instant. On the 12th, and after, visits will be made at private dwellings to search for wheat and flour that shall not have been declared. Quantities of these found will be confiscated.

(Signed,)   "GEN. COFFINIÈRES,
                    "*Commandant de Metz.*"

It was only now at this late date that the Maire of Metz issued a proclamation prohibiting that wheat flour or anything in the provision line, should go out of the city. News arrives from Paris representing the situation there more favorable. The report is spread that the lines of investment have been broken through, and that an army is marching to the relief of Metz. The public opinion is aroused to such an extent, that Marshal Bazaine publishes an article in the *Moniteur de la Moselle*, in which he says that he received no confirmation of the favorable news from Paris, and that he had never received the least communication from without since the commencement of the siege, in spite of his many attempts to establish relations. He closed this article by adding, that all should have confidence in his loyalty; that one thought and one thought alone should absorb all others —namely, the defense of the Fatherland; one cry should be upon the lips of all,—" Vive la France !"

However, this reply did not serve to better matters; for the people of Metz and the army had received several Paris newspapers announcing the downfall of the Empire and the proclamation of the Republic. At this time of starvation and excitement, the gallant Garde Nationale deemed that the moment to act had arrived. Nightfall came. The city was quiet and lugubrious, the rain coming down in a torrent; the wind had extinguished the solitary réverbère in the Place d'Armes. The great bell on the cathedral was rung. Several groups of the National Guard met on the Place de la Comédie; others more compact, march in the direction of the Hotel de Ville (City Hall) followed by a great throng of citizens, shouting, gesticulating, and flourishing canes excitedly. A company are on picket duty about the Mairie. Suddenly the peristyle of the Hotel de Ville is opened; men bearing torches descend, with slow step and grave faces, the great stone staircase. In their midst was the mayor, surrounded by all the members of the municipal council. The iron gates at the foot of the stairs were shut; they are now opened, and the crowd rush in. I followed, and was pushed and hustled along until I found myself right in front of the mayor. He was an old man; standing on the first landing, his hat in his hand. Every one uncovers; it is a solemn hour. The clock in the cathedral tower strikes ten. The mayor held in his hand a paper, the contents of which are as follows: " The National Guard wishes to assure Marshal Bazaine that he can count upon them. The municipal council will not in any way be answerable for events that have not been intrusted to their responsibility. The inhabitants must undergo privations equal to the occasion."

At the end of this speech the mayor expressed his great surprise that the supplies were so limited: he then withdrew, and the crowd dispersed. A copy of this was sent to General Coffinières, and another to Marshal Bazaine. The Marshal did not notice it: but General Coffinières replied, that the devotion of the National Guard was deserving of great credit; that the municipal council were in no way responsible, but that they in particular, and the people in general, ought to understand that when a population both civil and military, consisting of more than 230,000 souls, draws for two months from provisions intended only for Metz and the garrison (80,000), but little will remain; and, as the mayor said, all must " undergo privations equal to the occasion." This reply from General Coffinières was posted on the following morning.

October 11. No change in circumstances or bad

weather; no deaths in our ambulance; our coffee is at last all gone, and we are reduced to bad wine well diluted with worse water. We make our visit through the wards as usual. The cannonade continues, shaking the windows of my room as I jot down these lines. Fifteen of our out-wounded are again valid, and we send them back to their corps. Inside, our beds are all occupied, and likely to remain so for some time to come. In the streets I meet a few peasants, grocers, etc., carrying their last bags of grain to the Mairie, in accordance with General Coffinières' proclamation. For these they are to be paid at the rate of 30 francs a kilogram. About 4 P. M the rain abates and the clouds break up. At 7 the wind dies down and the sky is clear. It is again my turn to mount guard: this time I noticed a marked improvement in the discipline.

October 12. A bright sunny day; roll-call; everything is gone through with as usual; one death in our ambulance. The wounded in our tent are doing as well as can be expected under our reduced circumstances; the most were compound fractures of the lower leg, of the upper, of the arm, etc. The other officers tell me that the government officers are going about visiting all the houses, in search of grain, flour, etc. The pastry-cooks were the ones more especially honored. These had managed to hold out very well and always seemed, even in the most trying times, to have plenty of fresh cakes in their shops, which always found ready purchasers. This had not escaped the observation of the authorities, who now made a regular descent upon them, and, sure enough, found flour enough in all of their cellars together to last for *several days!* For this flour they none of them got a centime. It was a total loss and a just retribution.

Another case, where a man was rightly served, is the following one :

The theater of Metz belonged to a private company, and of course was suspended during the siege, the building remaining entirely unused. When the wounded began to pour into the city, every other place was soon filled up, and the surgeon-in-chief of one of the other ambulances applied to the company that he might have the theater in which to establish a temporary hospital. This was refused him. The theater remained closed; but once a week men went over the building inside cleaning it. This was continued to the end of the siege. The Prussians entered, and almost the first building they turn into barracks was the theater; in they went with wet mud, baggage, guns, etc. I stepped in once to see them, and they were lying about on the seats : some were playing cards and smoking in the Emperor's box; others were cooking their dinner on the stage, whither they had brought stones for that purpose; seats were overturned and broken; paint soiled, and gilding rubbed off. In the foyer, or green-room, was a surgeon dressing a wounded soldier who had a saber-cut across his head. The man was still under chloroform. The surgeon was very polite and showed me his work. The wound was sewed up with silver sutures.

At 6 P. M. I am relieved. It is already beginning to grow dark.

October 13. The roads are drying a little, and the fair weather continues. We learn to-day that a mysterious council of war was held on the 10th at headquarters. It appears that after an exchange of parlementaires, the enemy have accorded a *saŭf-conduit* to General Napoleon Boyer, chief of Marshal Bazaine's cabinet, who is charged with a mission for Versailles, the grand headquarters of all the German armies. General Bourbaki, commander of the Imperial Guard, had previously gone forth early in September under similar circumstances, but had never returned. General Boyer leaves; but few believe that he will come back. The forts are all silent again. It is a magnificent night.

October 14. The fair weather still continues. No change in affairs. In the afternoon, M. Liégeois is obliged to operate one of his wounded—a resection of the hip-joint. This is the only time we performed that operation during the siege. The patient lingered a few days and died. The city of Metz is becoming daily more and more excited. Translations from German newspapers have reached the inhabitants and troops,—telling of the Government of the National Defense at Paris, and the progress of the siege there. Nothing from our headquarters. Cries are raised against Bazaine; and the National Guard demand that the eagle surmounting the French flag shall be broken off. They visit the different public buildings, from which flags hang, and tear off with their own hands this emblem of the empire. After which they march to General Coffinières', and call him out. The general appeared on a small balcony, on the ground floor. A commandant of the National Guard, named Pardon, addressed him: "My General, in the name of the National Guard, we think it our duty to inform you that the population, piqued by the absence of all news, suspects the commander of the army of having information which he keeps concealed."

CHAPTER XX.

Speech on Behalf of the National Guard—A Visit to Café Infortuné—
The Execution—Our Party are fired upon.

THE commandant continued: "It is further desirable that Marshal Bazaine should make an act of adhesion to the Government of the National Defense, as his silence on that head has been remarked, and public opinion accuses him of preparing a capitulation in the interest of a Bonapartist restoration."

Two days later, General Coffinières declared, in presence of the municipal council, that he admired the great patriotism of the people of Metz, but that the fatal moment was approaching, and he wished to prepare them: he meant the fall of the city.

October 15. The usual morning routine is gone through with. The afternoon being fine, Mr. Mullet invites me to drive with him. He has succeeded in hiring a small wagon, something between a buggy and a cart. He could get no horse, and we took his (a saddle-horse) instead. While two of our infirmiers were harnessing up, they made various insinuating remarks about the turn-out, and seemed to think that the saddle-horse would not understand this thing rattling behind, and would become troublesome. All was ready, and Mr. Mullet, 2d Assistant Surgeon Brière, and myself got up. Away we went. The horse shied from side to side at first: we found that the blinders were the cause, and quietly cut them off, after which he went along tolerably well. We took the road up to Infortuné's, the little inn in front of

Fort St. Julien that I have before mentioned. Here we met Montebello, Charpille, and some other officers. Wine was at once ordered, and a grand spree commenced: drinking, singing, and smoking, dancing on tables, upsetting chairs, and breaking glasses seemed to be the order of the day—including, of course, making love to the barmaid, who was very pretty. She was evidently used to such goings-on, and appeared rather pleased than otherwise. Just as one of the officers had his arm around her waist, and was in the act of kissing her, the old father came in, and being much disgusted with the turn that things had taken, turned to the officer and upbraided him in warm terms—even going so far as to push him. The others seeing this, all got up, and, taking the old man to a window, pitched him out: he had not far to fall, and came off with a broken arm. It was now about 5 o'clock, and a major from the fort came in upon this drunken assembly, to tell the captains and lieutenants that they must return at 5:30, to be present at an execution appointed for that hour. A soldier having some spite against a sergeant, had come up behind him a few nights since, and sent a ball through his brain. He had been tried before a council of war, and condemned to be shot. We left Infortuné's almost immediately after, and went over to Fort St. Julien. On entering, we found a regiment of infantry—the 38th of the line—drawn up before the barracks. In their midst was a rude cart, to which was attached all that remained of a once good horse. This meager and dejected-looking representative of the equine race was well adapted to the mission he was about to fulfill. The officers bid us good-bye and joined their comrades, who, as usual, were talking together in groups near at hand. At about 5:25 the drums were rolled, and the regiment came to "attention."

The colonel galloped to the head of the column, the other officers fell into their places, and off they marched, the band playing a lively air. One squad, consisting of twelve men, remained behind,—this was the firing party. The wagon was now driven up to the main door of the barracks as fast as the horses would allow, and then the criminal came forth: he was handcuffed, and had a gendarme with drawn saber on each side: had he made the first movement that looked like an attempt to escape, he would have been cleft to the ground; and, had this have failed, the pistols worn in their belts would doubtless have finished him off. The prisoner was a very young man, and had probably committed the crime in a moment of thoughtlessness. He was assisted to the open cart, which contained an ordinary pine coffin. On this he was made to sit. The execution squad, which had remained at a little distance, were now motioned to, and drew near. The two gendarmes handed the certificate of death to the captain in command and withdrew. The captain disposed his men about the cart, so as to surround it completely, and gave the word "march." The cart, with its guard, rolled slowly out through the gates of the fort. I had remained, and, with Mr. Mullet, walked behind this funeral procession. Passing out, the cortége followed the walls of the outworks for some hundred yards, then turned suddenly in and descended a narrow lane, which lead down into the deep moats about the fort. This lane was very rough, and the wretched man was more than once thrown from his coffin onto the hard floor of the cart. On reaching the bottom of the moat, we followed the level for a short distance, the wheels sinking into slough. Suddenly turning an angle, we found ourselves in presence of the regiment. The soldiers were placed so as to form three sides of a square, the fourth being made by the high wall, a distance of about twenty yards intervening between it and the last men. The officers were all occupying their positions, thus leaving the inclosed space perfectly empty. As the *convoi* of death arrived, the lines made place enough for them to pass through. I remained outside, but could see perfectly well all that was transpiring. When the cart had arrived in the middle of the square, it halted, and the culprit was made to get down. The driver, throwing the reins over his horse, jumped from his seat, shouldered the coffin, and, following a soldier to a white post, laid it down in front; he then returned to his horse, and led him without the lines.

A Catholic priest who accompanied the prisoner, walking beside the cart and reading prayers from his breviary, now held a short conversation with him, and then commending his soul to heaven, he too withdrew without the lines. At this moment a soldier steps up and takes the condemned by the arm; he makes some slight resistance, whereupon several surround him, catch hold of him, push him and shove him with the butts of their muskets to the post of execution. To this he is tied, with his hands behind his back, and blindfolded. The captain in his turn comes forward, and in a loud but firm voice reads the death-warrant. Two soldiers then take knives from their pockets, and cut from his uniform all buttons, lace, stripes, etc. This is called the degradation. There is another grade of execution, in which the condemned are allowed to wear all these, also what decorations they may possess. It was impossible to see the entire expression of this man's face, as only the lower part was visible on account of the bandage; but I could trace deep sorrow and humiliation in the stiffly contracted muscles about the mouth. The condemned are supposed to be at their supreme agony when this is going on. This last task accomplished, the two soldiers returned to their comrades in the middle of the hollow square. The firing-party now advance to within twelve paces of the fatal post. Two ranks were formed, the captain standing on the right side. All was silent, and every eye turned upon the condemned. Not a word more was spoken or any command given; the captain nodded to his squad, who charged their chassepôts. This caused a rattling and grating sound that made the prisoner start. When this was done, and the squad came back to a shoulder, the captain drew his sword, and held it high in the air; at this gesture the muskets were aimed: he then brought it down to a salute; as the blade fell, the volley rolled out, and at the same instant the man, riddled with bullets, torn and bleeding, let his head fall upon his breast, and seemed to hang to the post. A battalion surgeon came forward and examined the body, which he pronounced not dead. A sergeant walked up to this mass of flesh and blood, and, putting the muzzle of his musket in the ear, fired. The skull was lifted, and the brains flew out in all directions: it was a horrid sight. This is called the *coup de grâce*. Among the twelve soldiers who formed this firing-party one was given a blank cartridge. Who this one was was never known. Such is the custom. As there is no difference in appearance between the real cartridge and blank one, each soldier may thus think himself free from bloodshed. The *coup de grâce* given, the body was cut down. The squad returned to their company, and "*Portez armes!*" rang down the lines. The soldiers fell into marching column, and, to drum and bugle, the whole regiment filed past the body. They turned the angle of the ramparts and disappeared, the last rays of the glowing sunset striking their bayonets. The heavy guns from just above our heads were booming at intervals. Mr. Mullet was deeply interested, and took a pull at his brandy-flask, this being by no means the first he had taken since we left Infortuné's.

In a very few minutes four men with spades came. They belong to the *génie*, and were jolly fellows, to which fact their red noses and jocosity bore evidence. Two of them stooped down, picked up the mangled remains, and dashed them with great force into the coffin, the lid of which they fastened carelessly with a few nails. The other two, singing all the while, had been engaged in digging a grave just deep enough to hold it. When this was done they let the coffin drop, as if it was a stone, into the receptacle made for it, which they filled up with a few spadesful of dirt. They then pulled up the post to take it with them, and, shouldering their spades, went two-by-two singing in chorus "La belle Venus." The strains of this comic *chanson*—which was, to say the least, *mal à propos*—died out, and left us alone standing before the grave.

Mr. Mullet took another pull at the brandy-flask, while I made a little note of what had happened; then we left the moat and ascended to the road.

We went straight back to Infortuné's. Here we rejoined our friend M. Brière, who assured us that he had witnessed the execution from one of the bastions. Presently the officers came back to finish their frolic; but, as the hour was getting late, we concluded to leave them, and return to Metz before the gates should be closed. That all were very tight, to say the least, may be readily understood. We bid the maid of the inn farewell, and went together to the small stable behind the house, where we had left our horse and wagon. We had unharnessed, and now experienced some trouble in getting on the gear. Brière wanted to put the horse's collar on over his tail, and Mullet wished to hitch him behind the wagon. After fussing and fooling for nearly an hour longer, we managed to get the animal in his right place, and, shouting out a good night to the officers, dashed off at a round pace down the hill. Mr. Mullet was driving. First we went to one side of the road, then to the other, —bouncing over stones, jumping across knolls,—the nag on the gallop, and each one holding on for dear life. We spoke to our reckless driver, who only replied that if " he broke our necks, he would break his own too."

About half-way between the fort and the city is a small hamlet, from which the former takes its name. Here was stationed a post, through which we sped. They shouted to us to halt, but received no more attention from us than if they had not have spoken. Just as we sank below a small eminence on this side, I thought I saw one of the pickets aim at us. I was not mistaken, for almost at the same instant I heard a report, followed by the whistle of a ball, that passed directly over our heads and lodged in a tree only a few yards in front.

CHAPTER XXI.

Fooling the Guard—The Bogus Wounded Man—Extracting a Ball—Death and Disease—The Army of Relief.

ON we flew over the level ground that we had now reached at the bottom of the hill, rumbled over the suspension bridge across the Moselle, and were not far from the Metz gate, when crash!—our left shaft came into collision with a hay-rack that had been left in front of the slaughter-house which we were just then passing. It broke in two in the middle: the piece flew back and struck me a severe blow across the head, which knocked me from my seat into the bottom of the wagon. By the time I had picked myself up and regained my seat, the vehicle halted, and we found ourselves at the drawbridge over the moat of the city fortifications. This was up. Several gendarmes and pickets who were occupying a small roadside drinking-shop hard by, came forward, and asked us what the matter was. We told them that we could not get in, and they recommended us to follow the walls around and try the next gate.

Seeing the handkerchief that I had tied about my wounded head, one of them asked me if I had been shot at the fore posts. We drove on again, keeping as near as possible to the walls. There was no road, and we were obliged to seek our way slowly over the open field. We had not gone far when we arrived in the midst of a cavalry camp. The sentinel seeing the red cross on our arms, allowed us to pass on. The soldiers had mostly retired to their tents, in many of which lights were burning; and I could see some of them, as the wagon moved along, sitting on the bare ground, writing upon their knees. These were evidently letters for the balloon post, which, notwithstanding the interrupted communications, functioned, leaving Metz every day at noon precisely, a cannon being fired to announce its departure. It was a paper balloon, and to which was attached the package of letters constituting the air mail. The weight of each mail could not exceed three-fourths of a pound. The post-office was a room in the Hôtel de Ville, occupied by several officers of the Intendance, whose duty it was to read all letters, and allow nothing that spoke of the sad situation to be sent. The letters had to be written on a piece of tissue paper two inches long by one inch wide (on so-called cigarette paper). When all was in order, the package was tied up with a wire, and fastened to the small metal ring at the neck of the balloon, which was then cut off from the inner court of the Hôtel de Ville; none being present save those in charge. The Prussians soon found out what was going on, and listened every day for the cannon-shot. They would then spy the balloons and shoot at them: sometimes they were low enough to be within range, and would come floundering to the ground; when they would pick up the letters, and finding nothing in them save a few words for a mother, a sister, or a brother, send them on, through their lines, to the south. At other times these balloons would go to a distance of twenty or thirty miles before coming down; farther than this we never heard of their going, although they were intended for journeys of ten times that length. Most of them were lost; the few that were not, all fell into the enemy's hands.

Around the large fire in the middle of the cavalry camp sat, on logs, some officers, smoking and talking.

We stopped, and asked them if they thought it worth while for us to proceed. They replied, "Oh, yes; go to the gate and say you have been to any village near here after wounded." Again we drove on, and after passing a second camp, began to approach the Porte de France. Mullet motioned me to lie down, full length, in the wagon, which he now halted on the edge of the fossé, and cried out, at the top of his lungs, to a solitary sentinel who was pacing the bastion above the gate. The sentinel charged us; and Mullet told him he had just come from St. Julien with a wounded man, which was indeed true, and wished him to open for us. He disappeared, and soon we heard the bolts drawn, and the massive doors were thrown open. Then the draw was slowly lowered, and we rode in. Several soldiers bearing lanterns now crowded around the wagon to get a look at the wounded man. One of them held the light just near my face, and discovered my uniform. Mullet's red face and broad grin, followed by Brière's titter, made me laugh outright, and the guard saw at once that we had taken them in. They concluded to pass it off as a good joke. We left them to enjoy it, and started off at our old pace, for the stable where Mullet had got the vehicle. We found this closed, and, unharnessing, left the wagon and gear before it, while one of us led the horse back to the Jardin Fabert. It is 10 o'clock; the stars are shining brightly, but there is no moon; we retire to rest.

October 16. Two deaths from pyæmia: one was a grenadier of the guard, who had received a ball in the upper part of the thigh, fracturing the femur in the superior third at the point of junction between the diaphysis and the head. Both were mashed and torn to pieces, in addition to which the many splinters had made a frightful wound in the muscular substance. The only choice left us was an exarticulation of the hip-joint; but, under the circumstances, the man having lost much blood, and being naturally of a weak constitution, this would have, perhaps, hastened the death that was surely awaiting him. Dr. Lefort spoke to him about his condition, and proposed the operation as a small chance: the patient refused, and, of course, we could not take it ill that he preferred so to die.

In my tent is a soldier of the line, who was wounded at Gravelotte, now nearly two months ago. The ball had entered the inguinal region, grazing the under border of Poupart's ligament; had passed down through the cellular tissue situated between the arteria femoralis and nervus cruralis, and lost itself. We could trace its course as far as the fascia lata only. Upon several repeated occasions we had made searches for the ball, which we had as yet been unable to find. To-day we put the man under chloroform, and commenced another examination with no success. The patient was doing well, and the wound progressing favorably. This afternoon, at about 4 o'clock, he complains of a feeling of heaviness in the sole of his foot. This we look at, and feel a hard substance. On making an incision we found the ball lodged just under the fascia plantaris. The patient had never complained of any pain since the wound was first made. He is convalescent, and will doubtless pull through.

The conduct of the wounded men, in general, was praiseworthy. They were patient and resigned; while that gaiety, so peculiar to the French character, never seemed to desert them. The two priests were busy giving them books, papers, tobacco, etc., and endeavored to amuse them as best they could; always reminding them of the trials and privations of Him who died for them.

The small-pox made its appearance about this date. One case in our tent was sent to a tobacco manufactory, where all others likewise affected were to be placed. On that same day two more arrived. This hospital was then given to the civil physicians of Metz; other sick came from day to day, and at the end of the siege five were still there; ten had been received in all, five of whom had died.

Dysentery was rapidly gaining ground. The offal, etc., thrown continuously in the river, doubtless helped the infection in its march of destruction.

The city and the army are at this moment enlivened by a ray of hope. On all sides they speak of a heavy cannonade heard during the night, and the officers of the Forts St. Julien and Quentin affirm that a battle was taking place in the direction of Pont à Mousson, beyond Ars-sur-Moselle; they had heard at intervals the distinct noises of mitrailleuses, and had seen *obus* fall in the Prussian camp at Ars. The officers made a detailed report on the different things that had come under their observation, and gave it to Marshal Bazaine. All the rest of the day and evening a movement on the part of the troops is anxiously awaited. The Marshal at first guarded his usual silence, and was not of the opinion of some fanatics that these signs meant relief; although a few soldiers, who, it is said, had crossed the lines, declared that the franc-tireurs of the Vosges had retaken Nancy, and that all along the route peasants had repeated to them, "Say at Metz that they must hold out: an army is coming to raise the siege!" This created a momentary spasm of joy, which was soon dissipated by the response of Marshal Bazaine: "I know what cannonade that is: the enemy are commencing the bombardment of Thionville."

Speaking of this reply, the report of the municipal council, which is filled with comments against Bazaine, says: "The army that was marching to our relief only existed, it is true, in the imagination of some unfortunate ones too prompt to accept the illusion that made them live again; but, in any case, the noise of cannon upon the night in question, came most certainly from a point directly opposed to Thionville. We are at present able to state that, in reality, a cannonade took place on the night of October 15. It was the bombardment of Verdun, which lasted from the morning of the 13th to daylight on the 16th."

No doubt was longer entertained as to Marshal Bazaine's having renounced all idea of attempting another sortie: moreover, every one believed that he had entered into negotiations with the enemy, and discussed the conditions of surrender. Some even went so far as to say that the Marshal had been over into the Prussian lines, and dined with the Red Prince on more than one occasion. The forts now maintained a sort of silent truce, and our troops went marauding between the lines; the enemy did not fire upon them: however, a few days later, I saw an old woman, standing a few steps from me, killed by them while digging for potatoes.

October 17. Duties as usual; the rain has not come back, but the sky is overcast; one death. Our out-patients are doing well; those within are finding it difficult to hold their own.

After the afternoon visit, I mount Lessy and start off, through the Porte de France, across the Pont des Morts, into the plain of Thionville. The graves of eight days ago had entirely disappeared. The camps about seemed to be in a state of apathy. No music, such as we used to hear early in the siege, enlivened them; all were quiet and downcast. I saw some six or seven soldiers standing about a dead horse by the roadside, and cutting off slices of meat for cooking purposes. Arriving at the pickets, I noticed that they too seemed to be negligent and sad. I got down from my horse and tied him to a tree. They asked me to draw near their fire, which I did. Their chassepôts were all stacked in the bushes, and only one man was on guard. After conversing for some time about the situation, one of the men said he thought, and all the army thought too, that Bazaine was a traitor: he asked me my opinion. I told him that I did not consider him exactly that; for when he took command of the army, the provisions were even then small.

CHAPTER XXII.

Entertained by the German Pickets—The 80th of the Line—A Night in the Elders—The Signal Lights—Morning—A Brush—Return of General Boyer.

IN continuing my conversation about Bazaine, I further said that the ammunition had all been shot away after the five days' fighting in August; that the Marshal owed his position and fortune to Napoleon; of this he was not unmindful, and would do all in his power to show the Emperor some return. For this reason he refused to recognize the Government of the National Defense. He would doubtless capitulate, and perhaps rather liked to do so, as he thought that thus he might, at least indirectly, aid the prisoner of Wilhelmshöe; but the reports about selling the city for gold, which some had circulated and many believed, were simply ridiculous.

Here the conversation turned upon other subjects. Presently I saw a Prussian picket, about eight hundred yards distant, come from behind a tree, throw away his gun, and walk toward us. He came up to our fire, and had in his hand a large piece of fresh beef and some pork. This he gave our pickets, and told them that he was sorry to see them in such a deplorable state. He was a sturdy, well-built fellow, with rosy cheeks and bright eyes, the very picture of health. He talked with us for some time, and then went back, inviting our men over to his post to take something. Just before he left, he said, "It is all over; Metz will be ours in a very short time." After he had been gone some ten minutes, our sentinel threw down his musket, and taking a comrade and me with him, advanced. We left four behind to take charge of the post. We crossed the field and came to a lane, along which was a row of trees (the Prussians had not cut down all the trees in their reach), and on the other side a trench. We climbed this, and found behind it a squad of eight men, all robust and fine-looking, sitting around a fire; four more were acting as sentinels. They all arose and shook hands with us, gave us some of their soup, a drink of good cognac, and cigars. They said that they, too, had suffered much from cold and fatigue, and were glad that the "swindle," as they called it, was coming to an end. We spent an hour together, and then returned to our lines. I was much pleased with the behavior of these German soldiers.

Mounting my horse and bidding the pickets good-bye, I galloped off and reached the St. Julien road. About half-way up, in a small defile, I could see a great mass of green bushes, brushwood, etc., filling the whole way, and moving slowly toward me. I thought of "Great Birnam wood coming to Dunsinane." The soldiers carrying this were completely concealed, and only became visible when quite near me. The effect was very peculiar.

I turned off and mounted the hill-side to the camp of the 80th of the line, in which my friend Montebello was serving. He told me that a few days before, he and Mullet had been over to Charpelle's camp, and that while they were there the Prussians had sent in a few shells. Mr. Mullet, who was always speaking of his great courage, was so overcome with fear that he forgot to throw himself upon his face, and fell on his back, thus exposing himself. Montebello asked me to stay and sup with him, adding that it was his turn to be on grand guard, and that I must come out with him. I accepted.

Dismounting, I gave my horse to one of his soldiers, and followed him by a narrow path around the edge of the hill on which the camp was. Here we found the colonel and several other officers sitting at a table constructed of a board supported by two drums. On this was supper—fever bread and bad horse—which I did not partake of, telling them that I had had a dainty morsel with the Prussians only an hour ago. After supper, a good fire was built just near, and we sat there for some time. Darkness had come on, and the *diane* was sounded. We then broke up, and each went to his own quarters, except Montebello and myself, whom the colonel invited into his tent. It was the largest and best single one I had seen, being of sufficient height to allow us to stand up. It was of conical shape, on the plan of an Indian wigwam, and contained his cantine bed, a military blanket and overcoat; while his sword and a large ten-barreled revolver were suspended from the pole that supported it. It also contained a small wooden table and two camp-stools. On the former was a map, field-glass, and writing material. The tent held us with ease. The table was cleared, a pack of cards produced, and, as a great treat, bad cigars and worse rum. We played ecarté, talked, sipped our liqueur, and smoked, until about 11 o'clock, when we rose to leave, as Montebello expressed a desire to take some repose before midnight, the hour appointed for the departure of the grand guard. On reaching his tent, which was like that used by the common soldiers, I could not help noticing the very small space it afforded within. We were obliged to crawl on our hands and knees through the mean aperture in front. Montebello lent me his blanket and overcoat, while he contented himself with his sheep-skins. We stretched ourselves out, and being very tired, were soon asleep. It seemed but a minute later when one of the soldiers came to wake us. We heard the cathedral clock toll twelve strokes as we stepped out in the dark, clouded night. The battalion that were to march were drawn up near the tent, and a commandant was calling the roll, a soldier holding the lantern for him. This finished, each captain read out his orders to his company (five companies making a battalion). The muskets were then loaded, and each company filed off, marching *à volanté*. We went straight up over the hill along the road, passing Fort St. Julien on the south side, and over the battle-field of the 7th. We were stopped twice: once at the fort—the sentinel knowing us almost immediately did not even ask for the word. This I thought very strange; for, suppose that we had wished to desert, nothing would have been easier. The other sentinel, at the little redoubt just beyond the fort, and on the other side of the road, was scarcely more particular than the first mentioned. About one hundred yards in front of this, and in a field, the battalion halted. Then they separated as follows: two companies went into the meadow beyond Merz; two into the woods at the other end of the village; and Montebello's company advanced to where a row of high elder bushes crossed the field. Here we stopped. The company was detailed in squads, who concealed themselves among the elder. They then sat down to see what would happen. All was still for nearly an hour, when we saw a man walking hurriedly along a cross-road not three hundred yards from where we were. The soldiers called Montebello's attention to this, but as the man was entirely alone and unarmed, he took no notice of him.

Time wore on wearily enough. About 2 o'clock we saw a light, large and bright, that appeared to be about half a mile distant, and carried by a man who was running along a mountain side. At first we thought this an optical illusion, as we knew that there were no mountains anywhere in that part of the country; moreover, a fog was filling the atmosphere at that moment. By chance, one of us happened to turn around, and, looking in the opposite direction, saw on the high ground beyond Metz a similar light. This one vanished and re-appeared thrice. Turning again to see the other, it was gone, and we saw no more of it. All were now convinced that these were signals.

Shortly after this I laid down in the bushes and went to sleep, not waking until daybreak.

Two or three dragoons then came up and rode past us. They went out in the field beyond the elder-trees, to a point where it goes down a steep hill, on the brow of which they halted and looked toward the enemy, holding their reins in one hand and grasping their loaded carbines with the other, resting the butts of them upon their saddle-bows, ready for use at a second's warning. After remaining there a minute or two, the dragoons turned north in the direction of the main route, on which was a small isolated house. When they neared this, they again stopped and looked, and shortly after came back to us, saying, "We have seen them. There is a company just down the hill, and another behind the house." The réveille was being sounded, and the camps all about were lively with the first signs of returning day. At this moment several of the Prussian pickets appeared above the hill and fired a volley at us, wounding two and killing one of our men. As I had on Montebello's military coat, I asked a soldier to lend me his musket. This he did, and I laid down behind an elder-bush to watch for a shot. Presently I saw three of the enemy on the brow of the hill. They fired at some of our men standing about one hundred yards from me—whom they could not see. This gave me time to take good aim, and I had the satisfaction of bringing one of them down; the other two disappeared. Presently I saw my man, who it seemed was only wounded, crawling away. I did not wish to kill him, so let him escape.

It was now time to return to camp. The company was mustered, and we started back. As we were leaving, a lively skirmish began between the two companies who had occupied the woods and the German post in front. The three dragoons who had gone over to reconnoiter unfortunately found themselves between the two fires; and I could see them fall one after another as they were picked off by the sharp-shooters. The horses were none of them touched, but turned and galloped back to our lines. The firing only lasted for a minute, when the two companies came out of the wood minus ten men. The companies from Merz likewise appeared; the battalion formed and marched back to the camp. The commandant reported to the colonel, who was just getting up after a good night's rest. He wished me *bon jour* and offered me a cup of hot coffee, which was very acceptable in the cool of the morning. This he said he had left over from his private supply, adding that if Bazaine did not hurry and make arrangements with the Prussians he should be obliged to come down to wine and water, like everybody else. I took leave of the colonel and Montebello, mounted my horse, and got back to the ambulance at roll-call.

October 18. Everything goes on as usual. No deaths to chronicle. The heavy clouds have not dispersed. Early this morning we learn of General Boyer's return, upon which the people and the army did not count. This morning an inspection of ammunition and reserve provisions was held. What the result of the interview of General Boyer, Bazaine's envoyé, with Bismarck and Moltke (the head and right arm of Prussia, as they were styled by the French), had been, no one then knew; but all soon found out that they were slowly but surely approaching the final catastrophe. It was only after the siege that we were able to read in the foreign newspapers what had transpired. I copy as follows from the *Indépendence Belge:* "All the intrigues which preceded that day, forever dark in our history, and that will weigh so heavily upon our destiny, had been arranged verbally between the generals and officers who had received the sad task of preparing the army. One day, in each brigade there was a reunion of the corps of officers; and we give, as nearly as possible, the terms in which the generals posted the troops with regard to the negotiations entered into by a marshal who thought the best manner of using 170,000 brave men was to place them under the walls of a city that was able to defend itself alone. The marshal authorized the generals of division to make known to the army the important events of the last three weeks. The store of provisions had, by a very rapid gradation, decreased at Metz."

CHAPTER XXIII.

Reply of the Prussians—Eating the Last Horses—Execution of Schull—A Medical Envoy to the German Lines—Firing upon and Wounding of the Same.

THIS article continues: "The army and the city were on the point of starvation; the generalissimo judged it useful, necessary, to open relations with the Prussians. He chose General Boyer as plenipotentiary and extraordinary ambassador. The general was his aide-de-camp, and, at an advanced age, had recently been promoted from colonel of the staff. He went to Versailles, to the grand headquarters of the sovereign of Prussia. An extreme ardor on the part of the enemy signalized that journey; and it would have been easy to draw a consequence in the interest of the French, as it showed beyond a doubt that the need was also experienced by the Prussians of making peaceful arrangements, and of ending hostilities. In order to facilitate, for example, General Boyer in the accomplishment of his mission, the Prussian government, master in France, had even suppressed, or at least intercepted, the regular railroad trains, in order to accelerate the journey of the Marshal's envoyé as far as Château-Thierry. Along the route from Metz to that town they had, it is true, with some complacency displayed the fantastic tableau of Prussian forces, scattered by groups and with art, at all points; and exaggerated, perhaps, after the fashion upon which the pasteboard men and villages that peopled the steppes of Russia were represented to the Empress Catherine.

From Château-Thierry a carriage bearing the arms and livery of His Majesty William, and which was awaiting the important personage, bearer of peace or war, transported him to Versailles with a vertiginous rapidity that again implied a certain desire to near the hour of treating.

"At Versailles, Boyer is immediately placed in conference with M. de Bismarck, who delineates to our envoy a frightful picture of the situation:

"Paris is given over to anarchy; and disputes, arms in hand, a power that Rochefort wishes to usurp, and that Trochu defends badly.

"France is not better off. Certain cities, abandoned to the disorders of socialism, have come to ask for Prussian garrisons;—the elections could not take place, the emissary prefects of the so-called provisionary government having reported that the population are far from coinciding with the new views; that this will be a check upon the Republic, and that no one would even go to the polls. Never was a more gloomy panorama unrolled.

"General Boyer is certainly of a weak mind, and easily accessible to reflexes. It is sure that he translated word for word, and with a most candid fidelity, the version given him. During this glacial representation of affairs, the King was informed of his arrival; and the first cold water having been thrown by the Prussian minister, General Boyer was received in royal audience. What am I saying?—in audience! The hall was full: a grand council of war was being held! The King was presiding, having at his right hand the Crown Prince: all around stood the highest officials of the German empire—Count Moltke at their head.

"Speak, General!"

"Timidly he exposes that the French army is very sick and miserable: M. de Moltke cuts the discussion short, and takes the word to decide, with a nicety of steel quite Prussian, that the question is military, not medical; the army of Metz must make for Prussia a second edition of Sedan,—it must surrender.

"M. de Bismarck, seeing that Boyer did not take to capitulation gaily, and that the intervention of Moltke was not exactly the kind of sugar that would catch flies, interposes. He, on the contrary, considers the question political. He would be disposed to accept a convention permitting to the army of Metz to retire where it should judge best—but in France,—on the condition of protecting the independence, as well as the order of votes and deliberations of universal suffrage. Thereupon they recapitulate on the absolute apathy of France,—of Paris that will not listen to reason,—of starvation,—of the approaching fall of the Government of National Defense, —of balloons,—of the red flag,—of the need of restoring public order.

"Then, as no government is more fitted to calm this anarchy than the one that excited it, they propose, instead of the actual government, the Empire represented by the Empress regent, under the safeguard, the protection of a marshal sufficiently indicated. If—that which was impossible (a Bonaparte caring more for a throne than for honor)—the Empress refused, recourse should be had to universal suffrage; and how could the universal suffrage take place better than under the shadow of bayonets? Such is the *rôle* left the army of the Rhine. The affair must be broken mildly to the soldiers; they are to understand that they will cover themselves with glory by firing when necessary upon their fellow-citizens."

The above is not the entire article, but I have cited sufficient to show what transpired at Versailles, and the position of affairs in general. Although it is in some passages rather equivocal, reports have since proved the authenticity of the statements made. It was thus, in lulling Bazaine to sleep with dreams of power, that Prussia was making us eat our last horse. Immediately a council of war is held. General Boyer recounts all that happened, and exposed the situation of France as it had been represented to him. The army of Metz could leave with arms and baggage only under the conditions named by the enemy. It was decided, by a majority of seven voices against two, that General Boyer should return to Versailles, and from there go to England, in the hope that through the intervention of the Empress Regent the King of Prussia might be disposed to give more favorable conditions to the army of Metz.

October 19. The state of the city is terrible. The sad end is approaching. On the Place d'Armes, where all the inhabitants were obliged to go for the distribution of bread, a crowd could every day be seen of old men and women, some bearing children in arms, all sickly and emaciated. Around the slaughter-house, beyond the city, soldiers would station themselves, and look with wolfish eyes at the bleeding horse-meat: one I saw go in and beg a small bit, which he ate then and there. Our wine is beginning to go; our linen, compresses, and bandages are getting low, and requisition is made. I had to give up my white aprons, in which I always operated, and soon lost sight of them. One day, while changing the dressing of one of my wounded, I saw the little red initials, J. B. (our family mark), on one end of a compress. I felt satisfied that the apron had been turned to a good use. To-day we have three deaths to report,—none of these were in my tent. The rain that has been threatening for a day or two past has not yet fallen.

Much talk has lately been made about a spy having been captured in our uniform; and we are requested to cease visiting the fore-posts more than two at a time, and these must be on foot. In the afternoon I visit Charpille, and pass the night in his camp.

October 20. At daybreak Mont St. Quentin fired a few shots, and from the tent I could see the lurid glare against the dark sky, and hear the distant boom of the heavy guns. I left the camp, and returned to the Jardin Fabert in a fine rain. After going through my duties, I was strolling along in front of the Hôtel de Ville; presently I saw the gates open, and a tall man, of distinguished appearance, came out. He was handcuffed, wore a Tyrolean hat, and a Scotch plaid shawl thrown loosely over his shoulders. A squad of soldiers surrounded him. I inquired of one of them who it was. He replied: "Schull, the great spy; he has just been condemned to be shot at daylight to-morrow morning, and we are taking him back to prison." The rest of the day Schull spent in writing to his wife: he bought two bibles, one for each of his children. These he left with the jailer of the city prison, who described his bearing as gentlemanly and refined, saying that he could not help shedding tears when the wretched man handed him the books and requested him, with faltering voice, to please send them to his family.

October 21. The rain increases. I do not attend Schull's execution. It is reported in the little siege journal, and occurred in the ditch behind the Caserne du Génie;—the only difference between this and an ordinary execution being, that the condemned was made to kneel, and that the officer called out, "Load!—ready!—aim!—fire!" He was buried on the spot after having received the *coup de grâce*.

We go through the order of the day. The number of the out-patients is diminishing: their wounds still continue to heal well in spite of all. This is probably due to the fact that they were mostly slight, and that the patients were sufficiently strong to be out; moreover, they were old wounds, and had been made before the siege, being in a state of convalescence before our misery began. No deaths to-day. Dr. Lefort is very angry at having met several of our officers on horseback at the pickets.

An aide-de-camp arrives from Marshal Bazaine, bearing a note requesting us to go over into the Prussian lines and leave a list of all the enemy's wounded in Metz. Dr. Lefort, to whom the list had been sent in the note, replied that he would go at once. He chose me to accompany him, and ordered the horses forthwith. We left the city by the Porte de la Moselle (there were four gates in all—the Porte de France on the north, the Porte Allemande on the south, the Porte Serpenoise on the west, and the Porte de la Moselle on the east), and took the road toward Malroy. We found no difficulty in passing the lines on both sides, rode up to the chief of the German medical staff in Malroy, and gave him our list. He was very kind, giving us refreshments, and showing us over his ambulance, with which Dr. Lefort expressed great satisfaction. He informed us that he was constantly receiving fresh supplies of lint bandages and medicaments from the rear, and that they mostlly were furnished by the "Sanitary Commission." We inquired if he had French wounded, he replied "No." After spending a very agreeable hour, we left him. As we rode back, we could see Prussian soldiers on all sides: they were drilling in the rain and mud. We were soon beyond the last pickets, and struck into a brisk trot, the wind driving the rain in our faces. We had reached a place where the route began to rise, when suddenly I saw some muskets flash; this was instantaneously followed by several reports and balls, that whistled by between my horse's neck and my head. I had time to see that this came from behind a fresh mound of earth, about five hundred yards distant, on the left of the road; and the red caps that had appeared for an instant above it, convinced me that the French had mistaken us for Prussians. The noise caused by the balls frightened my horse. He shied, threw me into a small gutter formed by the rain, and ran away at full speed toward the French lines. I raised myself on my elbow from my watery bed to look after Dr. Lefort. I could not see him anywhere, and called. No answer. I then turned around (I had fallen with my back toward the French lines) to look for him, still remaining on the wet ground, knowing that if I got up I should probably be fired at again. I saw him some two hundred yards distant, walking in the direction of our lines; with his left hand he led his horse, while in his right he held his cap high above his head. I could not tell whether he was wounded or not; he was going very slowly. Happening to feel a burning sensation in my left upper arm, I looked down, and saw that the sleeve of my uniform was torn, and that blood was oozing from the hole. I examined it hastily with my finger, and satisfied myself that only the skin and a portion of the front part of the biceps' muscle had been torn away, inflicting a slight wound. The ball must have passed out under my bent arm (between it and the body) as I held the reins.

CHAPTER XXIV.

Lying in the Rain and Mud—French or Prussian—A Narrow Escape—Horse-meat giving out—Brutal Butchery—Revolting Scene—The Last Meeting—Ordered to Fort Quelen.

TAKING out my handkerchief, I bound it about the wound as well as possible with one hand. Finding it rather wet, I endeavored to drag myself from this gutter to a place a few yards distant where at least I should only have mud. Beginning to move, and lifting my eyes to look in the direction in which I had last seen Dr. Lefort, I found that he had disappeared, and in his stead four dragoons were galloping down at full speed toward me. As soon as they arrived on a level with me they all suddenly halted, wheeled, and aimed their muskets at me. "Are you French or Prussian?" cried one of them. To this I replied, "French." They then became more friendly, expressed regret at what had happened, and offered to aid me. One of them seeing that I was wounded, got down from his horse and insisted that I should mount and ride back while he returned on foot within our lines. The rain was coming down more furiously, and the gusts increased every minute. Drenched to the very skin, I reached the walls of Fort St. Julien at a round gallop. Here I found Dr. Lefort awaiting me: he held my horse and told me that the affair had created quite an excitement in and about the fort; and I could see officers telescoping me over the breastworks. As soon as the dragoon who had lent me his horse came up, I returned it to him, and mounting mine, rode off with the doctor toward Metz. Entering more fully into conversation with him, I remarked blood on his forehead, and asked him if he, too, had been hit. He said no; that he had struck on a stone and raised the skin slightly, but that was all: in dismounting hurriedly he had slipped in the moisture and fallen. We reached the ambulance well satisfied with our lucky escape. Dry clothes, with hot brandy and water, served to restore us a little.

October 22. No change in our situation or in the weather. It is my guard—a very weary guard it is. After the morning and afternoon visits, there is nothing to do but occupy a camp-stool on the wet ground between two sick men, and watch the rain dripping from the roof and sides of the tent.

October 23. Relieved from guard. It is difficult to keep the cold and wet from our wounded, as the storm howls through the tents and cracks in the board buildings. We have no apparatus for warming. The day goes by as yesterday went—monotonous and dreary. The horse-meat is beginning to fall short, and the following proclamation will show that although much complaint was made by the citizens of Metz, yet their meat, such as it was, was all obtained from the army:

"October 23. Proclamation of the Commandant-Superieur. Requisition of horses for public aliment. City of Metz. Subsistence. The General of Division, commandant-superieur of the fortress, considering that the army can not longer furnish the horses necessary for the alimentation of the inhabitants; that it is from this moment indispensable and urgent to procure them; decrees: Article 1. The horses existing within the city walls, as well as those in the suburban communes within the line of siege, are placed in requisition for the alimentation of the inhabitants. Art. 2. A mixed commission, composed of two municipal councillors, a veterinary, an under-intendant, and two officers, shall be charged to designate such horses as are to be successively slaughtered, and to fix their price. The sellers shall receive, when the horses are delivered to the proper authorities a *bon* that shall establish their rights.

"F. COFFINIÈRES,
"*Commandant de Metz.*"

It will be seen that the inhabitants received a compensation for the loss of their property.

At 2 o'clock the same day at least fifty horses—old, young, large, small, thin, sickly, blind, dirty, shaggy (you could count the ribs on each), were led to the Place de la Comedie, where the commission named in the proclamation were sitting about a table under the portico of the theater. The price was fixed as each owner led up his horse; and although the former sustained some loss, yet the prices given were, for the most part, fair and just. As soon as a horse was sold, the veterinary would step up and with a lancet split the left ear from the base to the apex. To this operation some of the horses were very unwilling to submit. It was allowed in the camps to take any horse from those destined for the butcher's knife, provided you put one in his place; and some who were ill-mounted, thus got very fine horses. Also those from the government having their left ear split, could be obtained. Of course they had to be bought from the butchers, who sold some of them for a mere trifle. When the last horse had been disposed of, the commission announce that another sitting will be held to-morrow at the same hour (2 o'clock), and withdraw.

One of the most disgusting and revolting sights it has been my misfortune to behold, was that of a horse-butchery. There were several of these about Metz—the place generally being an open field. The one I refer to was by the side of a brook, between which and the road was a space sufficient to allow about thirty horses to be tied and leave room for the butcher. This man looked like a brute. Around him the ground was deluged with blood and the entrails of dead horses, which his assistants were engaged in skinning. He was so covered with blood that an incrustation had formed on the clothes he wore, while his face, hands, and arms were so bespattered that if I had ever seen him again I could not have recognized him. He seemed to take a savage delight in putting on the blinder and breaking the poor animal's skull with a powerful blow from his sledgehammer; then he would take a huge knife from his belt and draw it with a sardonic grin across the throat of his fallen victim. Sometimes his bloody work would not go fast enough: then he would loose a horse, retire a few steps, and run forward to bury the knife to the hilt in its heart. He would now pull it out, and stepping back again would watch the blood spurt forth in a great red stream, until the horse, if he were able to gallop off a little way, would make a few plunges, sink down, roll up his eyes and die. Another amusement seemed to be to let a horse go and then pick him off with a musket. A squad of cavalry happening to pass, halted, and justly upbraided this butcher. I was in company with M. Brière: the sight was frightful, and we passed on up the valley to a neighboring camp. It took us some time to get over the disagreeable impression thus made upon us.

9 P. M. It is a dismal night. There is a reunion at Dr. Lefort's rooms. He occupies a suite of apartments in the Hôtel de Metz, whither once a week all during the siege he has been in the habit of inviting the officers

of our ambulance. Cake and wine, as long as they lasted, were served. We played whist and chattered. There was a piano in the salon, and several of our number were good musicians. These soirées were very agreeable, and I spent many a pleasant evening at them. Thither I now went. The conversation turned, as all conversation at that trying moment, upon the miserable situation. There was no music or cards that night, which something told us was the last upon which we should ever reunite under similar circumstances on earth. All sat silently around a table upon which was a printed communication, reading as follows:

"Colonels will inform their officers that—

"1. The most complete anarchy rules at Paris.

"2. Rouen and Havre have demanded Prussian garrisons to maintain order.

"3. The Army of the Loire has been beaten near Orleans.

"4. Prussia will only treat with the fallen dynasty; the regency shall be represented by Marshal Bazaine.

"5. General Boyer has gone to demand acquiescement of the Empress.

"6. The army will receive no rations to-morrow and day after. They shall receive meat and wine. The soldiers are requested not to complain : in three days they shall leave Metz with the consent of the Prussians to go and establish order in France ;

"7. The commanders of corps are requested to make numerous propositions for the medal and the cross.

"8. The officers receive to-day the pay for November ! *Metz, October* 23."

This was without any signature, and copies had been that afternoon distributed all through the army. I also learned that Marshal Bazaine had despatched M. de Valcourt, one of his aids, to the delegation of Tours with explanations in regard to the army and its critical position. I give this despatch, which had now been sent for the sixth time to Paris and Tours:

"Upon several occasions I have sent men, volunteering for that purpose, to give news of the army of Metz. Since then our situation has only become worse, and I have never received the least communication from either Paris or Tours. It is, however, urgent to know what is passing in the interior of the country and at the capital; for, in a short time, famine will force me to act in the interest of France and of that army.

(Signed),   "BAZAINE,
"*Commander-in-Chief.*"

All were dispirited and spoke but little. I remained until 11 P. M., when I crossed the street and entered the Hôtel de Europe. In one of the rooms a frolic was going on; the sounds of singing interspersed with the clinking of glasses, burst upon my ears as I ascended the stairway. Shortly after reaching my chamber, I heard the servant girl outside the door complaining to another that an officer living in the hotel, and one of the party, had dropped a Prussian helmet out of the window, and that it had struck her on the head, inflicting a severe wound.

October 24. The storm in the night was fearful; my shutters were banged to and fro until one of them was blown off; there is no sign of abatement. I go down to the ambulance to duty. The out-patients come as usual. One death is reported: this was in our tent. After the visits, I am ordered by Dr. Lefort to go up to the fort of Quelen, and ask if the medical officer in charge has any lint left from the supply sent to the fort at the beginning of the siege. I saddled my horse, and with M. Letendard started off. We reached the fort by ascending a long hill, our horses slipping back constantly. No sentinels were anywhere visible, preferring to seek shelter rather than expose themselves to the blasts of wind and rain. The fort of Quelen commands the south side of Metz, and was in a better condition than any of the others. Although the siege was drawing to a close, yet even this one was not yet entirely finished. It was mostly composed of earthen works, which were fast being washed away. The stone barracks were built right up against these high dirt walls, as if it was a part of them. A few half-starved soldiers were hovering around a fire in the basement. The guns and bastions were abandoned to the clerk of the weather. As we rode through the large inclosure within the fort, I could see in the distance pickets; an occasional shot was fired. The barn of Grizy and the château of Peltre, where yesterday a battalion attempted a small foraging expedition, are both burning, and the great volumes of flame look the more fearful against the black sky. Casting a glance around me, I saw the white flag and red cross above one part of the fort. Thither we turned our horses' heads, and a few seconds brought us to the door of the fort hospital. As there was no place for our horses, we were obliged to leave them in the rain. We entered through a small aperture a long low room, from the center of which hung a huge lantern. At the other end, sitting upon a bench and smoking, were two medical officers. There was not a vestige of anything or anybody else. This was rather a bad lookout for lint. However, the gentlemen arose as we approached and stated the object of our visit. They both laughed, and one of them said: "Dr. Lefort must be out of his mind! We have had nothing here: all our wounded and material were sent to the city early in September, and since then we have received none. You will find lint nowhere." They passed some remarks upon the bad management of the medical department.

CHAPTER XXV.

Wounding of Second-Assistant Brière—No more Gas—Silence and Sorrow—Liberation of Mr. Eustis—An Excision of the Elbow by M. Liégeois—Distress.

THESE officers held the same opinion as we with regard to our deficient organization. They offered us some oakum for lint. We accepted, and they led us into a large hall filled with old guns. In one corner of this was a pile of oakum. They gave us each a meal-bag, which we filled. After enjoying their hospitality, in the shape of sour wine and damp tobacco of the cheapest brand, we took our leave, having first tied our bags across our saddle-bows. It is strange that these two men had received orders to remain in the fort, when they might have been usefully employed in some of the Metz hospitals, at a moment when every man was wanted. Never during the siege was a soldier wounded in one of the forts, and had there been, such cases could have been sent at once down into the city ; and the unnecessary waste of surgeons, which existed not only in Quelen, but in all the other forts and works of defense, would, in this manner, have been economized. Away we went— the tempest at our backs. In passing Tibault, a farm, through which the route runs, and where a company were generally stationed on picket duty, not a soul was visible, while the yard was literally flooded with water. In the middle I could see a small heap of old Prussian side-arms and helmets. We were half-way down the hill when we were met by a train of mules, bearing fagots on their backs. A solitary soldier had charge of them, and was conducting them to the fort. As we passed, I had the outside of the road, leaving Brière next to the mules. As the last one plodded by I heard him cry out, "I am wounded." He pointed to his leg. I rode around to the other side of him, and saw the blood streaming from a deep gash, just above the knee, in the lower portion of the vastus externus muscle.

The bleeding did not alarm me, as the wound was on the outer side of the leg, and the greater arteries thus remained intact. He told me that it had been made by the blade of a knife, protruding from one of the bundles of fagots. He saw the instrument, but was too late to avoid it. I at once got down, took out my pocket-case, and sewed up the wound, he remaining on his horse, which he rode back to the Jardin Fabert, at least one mile distant. We were obliged to proceed at a slow walk, and when we arrived the water was running from our garments. Brière did not catch cold, and his wound did tolerably well. In a few days the Germans entered, and brought us fresh supplies, and he then became convalescent. It was now dark; and for the first time during the siege the street lamps were not lighted. During our absence the following proclamation had been posted:

"October 24. Proclamation of the Commandant-Superieur. Gaslight. Metz—Public éclairage. The General of Division, commandant-superieur of the city, considering that it is impossible to carry on the gas service, as coal can not longer be obtained, decrees: Art. 1. From this date, 24th of October instant, gas shall no longer be employed in the streets, public establishments, or private houses. Art. 2. The Mayor is charged with the execution of the present decree.

(Signed,)   "F. COFFINIÈRES,
        "*Com. de Place.*"

After supper I returned home in the deepest darkness. The stores, etc., were ordered closed at 6 o'clock. The only places left open were the cafés, which likewise closed at 9. Into one of these I went. It was well attended. The tallow candle on each table had for a stick a bottle, a wine-glass, or a carafe.

October 25. Silence and sadness prevail everywhere. This is the most dismal and woe-begone period of our siege. The rain seems determined to continue, and falls thick and fast, there being no break anywhere in the clouds that hang like a great lead curtain over us. No change. Two deaths in our ambulance. Misery and despair. Not a shot to be heard anywhere.

In the afternoon, while walking toward the Hôtel de Europe, I am met by Mr. Eustis. This gentleman looked pale and thin, and after a few words of compliment proceeded to give me his narrative. We left him two months and a half ago on the battle-field of Gravelotte. He said that when the retreat commenced he had endeavored to follow; but the confusion was so great, and the army went so fast, that he was unable to keep up on foot, and found himself falling rapidly behind. At this moment he was descending the hill leading down to Maison Neuve. An artillery ammunition wagon being blocked there, he asked permission to mount on the empty box. I omitted to state that he had picked up a musket and saber; the latter, belt and all, he had buckled about him, while he shouldered the former. Thus equipped, he got up on the caisson, and the road soon becoming free, was hurried along over water-breaks, stones, etc. He describes his ride as being so rapid that he could, with great difficulty, keep from being thrown to the ground, as there was no railing or anything to catch hold of. At length, much jolted, and more frightened, he jumped off, falling heavily. He then walked as fast as his bruised limbs would allow him, in the direction of Metz. Fatigue overcoming him, he profited of the opportunity to get up on a charrette, containing one wounded man. He sat in front of the driver, straddling the horse's rump, and placing one foot on each of the shafts. The driver was thus obliged to pass the reins under Mr. Eustis' arms, as he leaned back against him. In this position they arrived before the gates. As they entered, some gendarmes and a squad of foot-soldiers stationed there halted them. "Who are you?" said one of them to Mr. Eustis. "I am Charles Eustis, of America," replied he. "That won't work; get down," said another. Mr. Eustis got down, and the charrette passed on. He was led into a small guard-room, and examined. In reply to the question, "What are you doing with those weapons?" he said, "I picked them up on the battle-field, with the intention of returning them to the government; here they are." Two men were then left in charge of him, and the others withdrew, taking the weapons with them. They soon returned, handcuffed him, and led him off through the streets to the city prison. Here Mr. Eustis was left. He occupied a stone basement room, and was subjected to privations and wants of all kind, being left entirely alone in the cold and damp. He was allowed no books or writing material, his only pastime being to look through the iron bars of his cell at other prisoners, who, at times, were allowed to exercise in the yard. This unfortunate state of affairs had lasted until the afternoon of October 24th, when he was brought before a council of war, first having been made to stay three hours in the criminal waiting-room. At last his name was called, and he mounted the stairs trembling. In the judgment-hall sat seven generals, in full uniform;

on their right stood the Procureur-General, the secretary occupying a desk on the left. All were silent as he entered, and he assures me that he felt the gravity of his situation. The Procureur-General, without giving him time to reach the stand usually occupied by prisoners, came forward, and handing him a little note-book that had been taken from him for inspection, said: "Mr. Eustis, you are accused of espionage, also of having taken unlawful possession of French arms. We have investigated your case. You are acquitted unanimously." The poor man threw himself into the Procureur-General's arms and wept. There is no appeal from this council, and with them it is life or death. Mr. Eustis was deserving of great sympathy, but got no reparation for the unjust treatment he had received at the hands of the French government. He remained in Metz until it capitulated. The last time I saw him he passed me in a wagon in the Rue des Clercs: he looked out and said, "Good-by; I am going to Saarbrücken." A few weeks later I heard of his death, which occurred in a storm on board of a steamer, plying between Havre and Bordeaux. He died of small-pox, and was on his way to offer the Remington rifle to the Southern Army—was a man of great force of character, and zealous in the performance of his duty.

This is the last night of suspense. Before retiring, I am told by some officers conversing in the dining-room, that the Prince Frederick Charles had declared negotiations broken, and that an announcement to that effect had been made to the troops early in the evening. Moreover, the Empress had refused to combine with the authors of the proposed plan, and retired from the game. When Marshal Bazaine received this news, he forthwith held a council of war, in which he requested General

Changarnier to go to Prince Frederick Charles, in order to endeavor to obtain, not a capitulation, but an armistice, with a renewal of supplies, or a permission for the army to go to Africa. The Prince received the old general with courtesy, but stopped him at the first word, —he had not the capacity to treat. The Prince, on his side, had formal instructions: the army and city must surrender, without conditions, at mercy. General Changarnier had brought back this disheartening reply at 8 o'clock.

October 26. The worst is known, and all are now certain that the capitulation will very shortly occur. Roll-call as usual; and as all stood up in their places, the rain pouring down, emaciation and sorrow were painted on every face. M. Liégeois went down the list with a mournful voice, and I thought I could discover a tear in the corner of his eye. We went over the wards. Two more had gone to their last account. The number of out-patients is less to-day than ever before. In the afternoon M. Liégeois performs a resection of the elbow. A table, showing the number of operations performed during the siege of Metz, at the military hospital, was subsequently shown me: although I took no note of the number, yet memory serves me thus far, that I am able to state that the resections were most frequent. M. Liégeois' operation was upon a servant girl, in a family of his acquaintance. The arm was in every other way healthy. She gave, in the anamnese, that she had, some years ago, received an injury to that part of the right arm; this had been followed by inflammation, which had terminated in a bony anchylosis. She could move her hand but insufficiently, and had never been able to put it to her mouth: this was the more trying, as she also acted as cook. The operation consisted in excising the olecranon together with a wedge-shaped piece of the upper part of the ulna, as far as the lower extremity of the coronoid process. The mobility of the joint (the main point to be gained) was kept up; and when we left Metz, a few days later, she was doing well, and was given into charge of the family physician.

The distress at this date is beyond description. The horrible weather continues day and night. The camps are nothing but great masses of mud and water, where the wretched soldiers ate their coarse bread and horse-meat without salt, that they had hardly the courage left to cook and place it between their chattering teeth. They were ill-covered, and trembled with fever. The horses that had not been designated for the slaughter-house were dying at their stakes, or held in useless fetters, for, alas! they thought little of running away. In vain did those noble animals gnaw the bark of trees and the branches, still covered with dead leaves, dragging in the filth of the camps. Their strength was diminishing each day. They would also eat each other's tails off, as if to deceive their craving hunger. We saw them often—mere skeletons, with the skin worn off in many places—hang their heads in weakness, their eyes sunken and almost out, and fall down in the mud.

CHAPTER XXVI.

Last Resources—Capitulation of Metz—Protocole and Appendix—Riotous Scenes—Intervention of the Military—An Officer in Despair blows out his Brains—The Final Effort—A French Soldier's Knowledge of his Musket—Inspection of our Ambulance preparatory to the Surrender.

AT the close of the last chapter I was describing the pitiful position of the army horses. Some fallen ones would move themselves in a fruitless endeavor to get up, and then fall back again and die—stretching out their poor limbs. More than one trooper wept at the death of his favorite steed; and this heart-rending spectacle was repeated everywhere, at every instant. The horses of officers fared but little better. General Coffinières informed the inhabitants of Metz that he has thoroughly examined the situation; that there is not material enough to make an efficacious opposition; the last resource would not carry them beyond 30th of October instant; the siege could not be continued without provisions, and in a city overloaded with wounded: moreover, that he could not prevent the enemy from profiting of their advantages; and that city, army, and material must undergo the hard necessity of surrender. He closed his proclamation by saying that he would obey the orders of Marshal Bazaine. It was unanimously agreed in a council of war, "not without the deepest grief," says the summary report, that M. Jarras, general of division, should be sent to the headquarters of Prince Frederick Charles, as delegated by the council, and with full power to decree and sign a military convention, by which the

French army, vanquished by famine, should constitute itself prisoner of war. It was about 6 o'clock in the evening when General Jarras left for the château of Frescaty, a villa situated about five English miles southwest from Metz, where a conference was to take place between himself and General Stiehle, chief of the Prussian staff. The French general was accompanied by two officers of the grand staff, charged with drawing up the articles of the protocole as fast as they should be decided upon by the two plenipotentiaries. The Prussians having declared that they could not consider a difference in the fate of the city and that of the army, and the council of war having accepted that pretension, General Jarras had received the mission of treating for both. Thus the first article decreed that the troops under Marshal Bazaine were prisoners of war; the second, that Metz, with all contained in the fortress, should be placed in the hands of the enemy. The whole convention was comprised in these two articles; the rest was only an affair of detail : if those in command had not waited until the last distribution of bread, and had acted with energy at the outset, they might have, with the second article, obtained better conditions for the first. The discussion between the plenipotentiaries then turned upon a secondary question, viz : Should the officers keep their swords, and take with them their baggage? After an exchange of dispatches between Frescaty and Versailles, the last clauses were accorded; a slim compensation in such a sad extremity, and for officers who claimed to have done more than their duty.

October 27. The number of wounded in our outservice is falling off,—a few every day. Some are well enough to remain away; others are kept off by the bad weather which has settled upon us. Three more die in the wards. Duties as usual. At 2 o'clock in the afternoon General Jarras, in company with his two aids, rode over to Frescaty for the second and last time, and there signed, with General Stiehle, the capitulation of Metz, by which that city and army of 170,000 men became prisoners of war.

I here transcribe the "Protocole of the capitulation of Metz, between the undersigned, chief of grand staff of the French army at Metz, and the chief of staff of the Prussian army before Metz; both accorded full power by his Excellency, Marshal Bazaine, commander-in-chief, and by the general-in-chief, his Royal Highness Prince Frederick Charles of Prussia. The following convention has been concluded :

"*Article* 1. The French army placed under the orders of Marshal Bazaine is prisoner of war.

"*Article* 2. The fortress and the city of Metz, with all the forts, material of war, provisions of all kinds, also whatever is property of the state, shall be surrendered to the Prussian army in the same condition that they shall be in at the moment of the signing of this convention. On Saturday, the 29th of October, at 12 o'clock, the Forts of St. Quentin, Plappeville, St. Julien, Quelen, and St. Privat, also the Porte Allemande (Route de Strasbourg) shall be placed in the hands of the Prussian troops. At 10 o'clock on the day named, officers of artillery and miners, with certain under-officers, shall be admitted into the above-mentioned forts to occupy the powder magazines, and blow up the mines.

"*Article* 3. The arms, as well as all material, consisting of flags, eagles, cannons, mitrailleuses, horses, ammunition carriages, equipages of the army, supplies of ammunition, etc., shall be left at Metz, in the forts, in the hands of military commissioners appointed by

Marshal Bazaine, to be immediately given over to Prussian commissaries. The soldiers, without arms, shall be conducted, arranged according to their regiments or corps, and in military order, to the places indicated for each corps. The officers will then be allowed to re-enter, at liberty, within the trenched camp or Metz, under the condition that they will give their words of honor not to leave the place without an order from the Prussian commander. The troops shall then be conducted by their subalterns to places of bivouac. The soldiers shall keep their sacks, their effects and objects of encampment (tents, blankets, pots, etc).

"*Article* 4. All generals and officers, as well as military employés holding the rank of officers, who will give their written word of honor not to bear arms against Germany, and to act in no manner contrary to her interests until the end of the present war, shall not be made prisoners; officers and employés accepting this condition shall keep their arms and the objects belonging to them personally. As a recompense for the courage of which the army and the garrison have given proof during the entire campaign, it is also permitted to officers choosing captivity, to take with them their swords and sabers, as well as all that belongs to them personally.

"*Article* 5. The military surgeons, without exception, shall remain behind to take care of the wounded: they shall be treated according to the convention of Geneva. It shall be the same with all persons connected with the hospitals.

"*Article* 6. Questions of detail concerning principally the interests of the city, shall be treated of in an appendix, which shall be annexed to, and have the same value as the present protocole.

"*Article* 7. Every article upon which there exists any doubt, shall be interpreted in favor of the French army.

"Given at the Château of Frescaty the 27th of October, 1870.

    (Signed,)   "L. JARRAS,
                                                 "STIEHLE."

"Appendix to the military convention as regards the city and the inhabitants:

"*Article* 1. The employés and civil functionaries attached to the army or the city, are at liberty to retire where they wish, and take with them all their effects.

"*Article* 2. No one, either of the National Guard or of the inhabitants of the city, or of those who have sought refuge in the city, need be uneasy about the opinions, political or religious, that he may have held; about the part he may have taken in the defense; or the aid he may have given to the army and the garrison.

"*Article* 3. The sick and wounded left in Metz shall receive the care that their condition may demand.

"*Article* 4. The families that may be left by members of the garrison at Metz, need not be uneasy, and are at liberty to depart with all their effects, like the civil employés. The furniture and property that members of the garrison may leave behind them, shall neither be pillaged nor confiscated, but shall remain their own property. They can cause them to be forwarded within a delay of six months from the declaration of peace, or from their liberation.

"*Article* 5. The commander of the Prussian army engages that the inhabitants shall not be maltreated, in person or property. Shall equally be respected, property of all nature belonging to the department, the communes, to societies of commerce and others, to corporations, civil or religious; to hospitals and establishments of charity. No change shall take place in the rights exercised by corporations or societies, as well as by private individuals, toward one another in virtue of French laws, at the day of capitulation.

"*Article* 6. In this respect it is particularly specified that all the local administrations, societies, and corporations above mentioned, shall preserve the archives, books and papers, collections and documents of every description, that may be in their possession. The notaries and other ministerial agents shall also preserve their minutes and dépôts.

"*Article* 7. The archives, books, and papers belonging to the state in general, shall remain in Metz; and at the declaration of peace, all of those documents that refer to portions of territory restored to France, shall also be restored to France.

"Given at Frescaty the 27th of October, 1870.
 (Signed,)   "JARRAS,
                "STIEHLE."

These documents were posted in the streets and public places of Metz on date.

It was evening: the excitement and alarm created by their appearance was very great. People rushing about here and there, or standing in groups, one of whom would read to the others; while women and children were shouting, "We are Prussians! to death with Bazaine!" I happened to be passing the Place de la Cathédrale; a riot was attempted; a captain of artillery, at the head of a mob consisting of at least two hundred men, women, and children, armed with guns, pikes, spades, etc., were marching toward the Porte Allemande. They halted a minute, and the officer harangued them, inviting all to press forward and charge the Prussians. Bazaine's life was threatened. The bells all over

Metz were rung violently, and watch-fires built. This mob moved on; and shortly after the National Guard arrived, singing the Marseillaise. Nothing could be more lugubrious than the last moments of this sad drama; the population, so French, so patriotic, was exasperated at the fatal dénôument that had been so long awaiting them.

The rioters were soon quieted by the appearance of a battalion of the line, who had orders to fire at once if they did not disperse at the first roll of the drums. Such disturbances continued, would only have brought about useless complication, and have authorized the Prussians to commit excesses.

A good number of officers could not support the idea of such a capitulation. One of them blew his brains out. As I was entering the Hôtel de l'Europe, another was bidding the landlady good-bye, and saying: "Several high officers have succeeded in getting together a few thousand men; and we are going to cut a passage through the enemy's lines." I afterward learned that they could not agree, and that the project had fallen to the ground.

The *Moniteur of the Moselle* says: "General Cissy had offered to take command of that handful of brave men; but at the decisive moment he was nowhere to be found,—which fact astonished no one."

October 28. The army and inhabitants have cooled off a little—doubtless the rain aided them; and now seem to take things in a more matter-of-fact manner. Rollcall and duties are gone through with. Dr. Good, who was charged by Dr. Lefort (Dr. Lefort is the son-in-law of the great Malgaigne) to visit Marshal Canrobert, invites me to accompany him. The Marshal lived in a villa on the Thionville road: it could be approached from two sides. The guard did not know whether his liege and lord was at home or not. Dr. Good laughed, and asked him if he understood the use of the chassepôt: he answered, "Not very well." It turned out that the Marshal was absent in the city, whither we returned. One death in our tent. We sent off the last batch of those who were again valid, this morning. Our ambulance is visited and inspected by General Coffinières with two aids, in company with Dr. Lefort. Everything is put in order; lists of the wounded in each ward drawn up, giving name, regiment, etc.; and the final arrangements made preparatory to surrendering the 1st French Ambulance to the Prussian medical officers.

CHAPTER XXVII.

Bazaine takes Leave of the Army—A Traitor and his Accomplices—Arrival of the Prussians at the Porte Allemande—The Surrender—Marching into the Enemy's Lines—Their Medical Service—They patrol Metz.

A SIMILAR inspection was made in all other hospitals, ambulances, or depôts for wounded. The number of the latter was now reduced to 22,000, this being the figure given in the final French report. A momentary comparison with the statistics given in the first part of this work will show the frightful mortality that prevailed during the siege of Metz; and it is only a wonder that the plague did not break out. On this day Marshal Bazaine takes formal leave of the Army of the Rhine, in a proclamation, which I give as follows:

" *Order General No. 12, Army of the Rhine.*

" SOLDIERS:—Vanquished by famine, we are obliged to submit to the laws of war, and constitute ourselves prisoners. At different epochs in our military history, brave troops, commanded by Masséna, Kléber, Gourion St. Cyr, have had the same lot—which does not in any way blemish the military honor, when, as we have done, duty has been so gloriously accomplished to the extreme human limit. All that could possibly and with loyalty be done to avoid this end has been attempted without success. As regards the making of a final effort to break through the fortified lines of the enemy, in spite of your valor and the sacrifice of thousands of lives that can still be useful to the country, it would have been fruitless on account of the armament and overwhelming forces that guard and support those lines: a disaster would have been the consequence. Let us be dignified in our adversity; let us respect the honorable conventions that have been stipulated, if we wish to be respected as we deserve. Above all, let us avoid, for the reputation of the army, acts of indiscipline, such as the destruction of arms and material, since, according to military custom, city and material will be returned to France after the signing of peace.

"In resigning the command, I desire to express to the generals, officers, and soldiers, my gratitude for their loyal aid, their brilliant valor in battle, their resignation during privations; and it is with a broken heart that I leave you.

"Marshal of France, Commander-in-chief,
"BAZAINE."

The Marshal cites the examples of Masséna, of Kléber, and of Gourion St. Cyr. Articles were written, and a great outcry made upon this point. A small pamphlet, signed "An Officer of the Ex-Army of the Rhine," was circulated; and a copy found its way to our ambulance. It contained, among other things, "that in no country, at no time, had there been an example of such a shameful capitulation; of an army so numerous allowing itself to be shut up—to be starved out without having been beaten—without having made a serious effort to break the line of siege." Gabour's history of France shows us that Masséna was allowed to lead his army out with arms and baggage, with the understanding that he was to recommence hostilities as soon as he crossed the French frontier. Dorée confirms this, and states that Kléber left Mayence with arms and several cannon—

with this promise alone: that he would not serve against Prussia for one year.

Gourion St. Cyr only surrendered Dresden after a desperate resistance, having obtained permission to be reconducted to France with his troops. We know that this article of the capitulation was not executed, because the allies did not carry out their engagement. An article in the Metz *Courier* of October 28th closes by saying: "Marshal Bazaine is a traitor, and the generals who signed that infamous document his accomplices." It was touching to see the old soldiers, to whom the flags were always intrusted, plodding through the rain and mud, weeping and carrying these regimental palladiums to the arsenal, where the Prussians should find them. Several flags were burnt, but all, with the exception of these few, were delivered up. Marshal Bazaine said negligently, "These military trophies have no value unless taken on the field of battle." The Prussians did not seem to think so, as they ornamented their streets with them when their soldiers came back, and then took them to adorn the walls of their museums.

October 29. There is at last a break in the clouds, and the rain now ceases and falls again at intervals. We have our last roll-call; make our last visit through the wards of that ambulance that I shall always remember; register our last death; dress the few out-patients that come, and bid them good-bye; put the material, etc., in perfect order; and place the lists in the hands of M. Liégeois, whose duty it is to hand them over to the Prussian medical department. At 11 o'clock all is ready. The Prussians arrive at 12. All through the army similar scenes were being enacted; registers made; equipages arranged; accounts of stores written out, etc.: in short, the final steps taken preparatory to marching over into the enemy's lines. The hour left I passed in visiting the camp of the 3d Chasseurs, on the Thionville road. The mud in some places was so deep that my horse found difficulty in walking through it. My object was to take leave of a friend, a son of General Bixio, who was about to go with his regiment into German captivity.

As I returned to the Jardin Fabert, I could see the troops on all sides stacking their arms, packing up, and breaking camp. The enemy's flag already floated above Fort St. Quentin. As the clock struck 12, a Prussian battalion, the 1st of the 41st of the line, marched up and took possession of the Porte Allemande, in accordance with the terms of the convention. They arrived quietly and without music. This gate was being guarded then by a company of the 6th of the French line, who evacuated as soon as the captain had gone through the ceremony of handing over the keys to the German major. I have a very lively recollection of the 6th. One day, when they were encamped at Scy (it was early in October), I happened to pass a leisure hour in strolling through that village, which lies about three kilometres west of Metz, and at the base of Mont St. Quentin on the other side. I walked through, and soon found myself in a narrow lane between two high walls, over which I could make out the Prussian lines on the hills opposite. Stopping to contemplate them, I was touched on the shoulder by a soldier, who wished to know my business there, as it was forbidden ground. Somewhat surprised at being thus accosted, I produced my army card, and told him that he should be punished for his insolence. He smiled and called the guard. In a moment a dozen of his companions appeared, surrounded me, and led me back into the village to a house where their lieutenant was quartered. I explained to him my position: he seemed satisfied, and let me go. I started back toward Metz, congratulating myself upon having escaped any further inconvenience. Halting at an old inn, I heard the sound of a man running, and looking behind me saw another of the 6th coming after me. He said he was very sorry, but would I please to come back? I returned to where I had left the lieutenant, who it seems had spoken to his captain; the latter was now awaiting me. The whole village was alarmed: old men, women, and children, crowded around; laughing, taunting, jeering. "A spy! a spy!—he is certainly German!" was in every mouth. The captain, evidently being of the same opinion, gave me a leer, and then turning to his men, said, "Take him to the general!" A pair of handcuffs were slipped on me, and the soldiers again surrounded me, with fixed bayonets and loaded muskets. We went down a hill, crossed a field, and thus came to Longueville, the soldiers talking about my execution as we walked along. General Cissy was standing on the steps of the house that he made his headquarters, rolling a cigarette. In the garden in front a regimental band was playing "Sally come up." As the squad entered the band stopped, and all eyes were turned upon me. The sergeant halted us at the foot of the steps, and said: "General, we have captured this spy." I at once told General Cissy about the mistake. He was polite, expressed regret, and liberated me.

On a previous occasion I had likewise had the pleasure of being arrested by General Pardon; this time on the banks of the Moselle, in a camp just under the walls of Fort St. Julien.

Apologising for this digression, I return to the arrival of the Prussians at the Porte Allemande. After dinner, the different corps form and march off in the order designated. The whole army was divided into four divisions, each of which took one of the four roads leading from Metz. Although the medical officers were not obliged to march out with the troops, yet Dr. Good and myself preferred to do so. We went out through the Porte Serpenoise, and there joined Frossard's corps, who were already *en route*. The country about was flooded by the late rain and the overflowing of the Moselle; the mud and slime in the roads and meadows was such as I have never seen before or since. The troops marched along without any attention to order. They looked miserable; many were weak, dragging their weary limbs along as best they could; others would fall down and faint, while their comrades passed on into captivity. I saw several officers break their swords as they left the walls of the city, to accomplish the sad mission of placing in the hands of the Prussians the soldiers, vanquished and disarmed, that they had so often led against the enemy. It was a mournful and impressive sight; the soldiers bursting into tears and throwing themselves into the arms of their officers, who with difficulty kept back their sobs. Those men, habituated to contemplate death at every moment, were overcome with shame and grief; and I heard more than one deep imprecation upon the heads of those who had placed an ineffaceable spot on their military honor.

The first sign we had of the enemy was after half an hour's march, and just this side of Magny, in the shape of two Prussian gendarmes stationed by the road. Just beyond Magny, which lies to the south of Metz, a regiment was drawn up on each side of the route, while Prussian staff-officers were riding about. The hills and valleys far and wide were filled with German troops of all arms. As each French regiment marched up it was halted, and the colonel handed his list to the Prussian officer delegated for that purpose, and withdrew. The under-officers, after bidding their soldiers a last farewell, likewise withdrew and returned to Metz. As each regiment went through, a company of the German infantry would close in and march behind them. The surrender lasted until late in the afternoon.

While standing there viewing it, I had an opportunity of observing the medical arrangements of a Prussian regiment. I have stated that there were two: each of these had its little two-wheeled one-horse cart (above which floated the red cross), containing medicines, instruments, lint, bandages, etc. This was stationed at the flank, and a few dozen paces from the column; around it stood the regimental surgical corps, one hundred strong (a Prussian regiment consisting of three thousand men). Their system is as follows: the regimental surgeon has four assistants; each of the three battalion surgeons has likewise four assistants; the infirmiers are used as occasion demands with any particular division.

While the marching through was going on, a tremendous detonation announced that the Prussians had blown up a small redoubt just beyond the Porte Serpenoise; and now the vast volume of smoke and sand was sent high into the air, hiding for an instant the city from our view.

Metz and the forts are entirely in the hands of the Prussians. The army has gone. When we got back, their cavalry were patrolling the streets.

CHAPTER XXVIII.

Triumphal Entrance of the Prussian Army into Metz—Troops passing through—The German Medical Department take Possession of our Ambulance—Our Surgeons leave for Belgium—Dr. Good and Myself bid Farewell to Metz—En Route for the Army of the Loire—Scenes along the Way—Arrival at Gland.

THE fine appearance of the horses and men was a subject of remark by all. They were soon followed by several regiments that came up to the Place de la Cathédrale, with drums, fifes, and music; the black-and-white flag hanging above their bayonets. The stores had all been closed at 12 o'clock, and the inhabitants betook themselves to the streets. The city was filled with Prussians, who occupied the theater, the school of application, all the hotels, etc. It is 9 o'clock at night. For the first time the German's trumpets call the troops to rest within the walls of Metz. On returning to the Hôtel de l'Europe, I found the yard in front occupied by troops and baggage-wagons. Two sentinels were at the gate, and at first refused me entrance. It was only when I had succeeded in convincing an officer that I really lived there, that he allowed me to go up to my room under escort of two gendarmes.

October 30. The sky is still overclouded, but there is no rain. All night long, drinking and noise have been going on. Much excitement is caused among the Prussian officers in the hotel, because one of their number has been killed by a French officer, who chanced to meet him in the hall about midnight. The Prussian was intoxicated. The Frenchman, after inflicting the stab with his sword, made his escape by the servant's stairway. Whenever one or two soldiers are caught alone, they are beaten and wounded by the French. This state of things continued for a day or two only, until General von Kümmer posted a proclamation, stating that whoever should strike or steal from a German soldier should undergo the penalty of death. All the public places are filled with sutlers, provision-trains, beer-venders, tobacconists, etc., that followed the German army. They find ready customers for their fresh supplies of meat, eggs, butter, vegetables, etc., among the famished French. The statue of Fabert, in front of the cathedral, is covered with crape, and the French flag still waves from the highest pinnacle of the building. I go down to our ambulance, and find the Prussian medical officers already at their posts. They expressed much surprise at the manner in which some of our cases had been treated, but made due allowance for the trying circumstances under which we had labored. Ambulances belonging to the foreign branches of the Sanitary Commission now begin to arrive at Metz. Three came to-day. First, the English branch. This ambulance, under direction of Captain Brackenbury, made numerous and abundant distributions of objects of every nature to the sick and wounded. They established themselves at the Caserne du Génie, functioning until February 8th. Four hundred and sixty wounded were cared for, and generously provided with whatever was necessary. Second, the Belgian branch, delegated by the Central Committee of Bruxelles, and under the direction of M. A. Vischers. This ambulance established at the Convent Saint Christian, functioned until the 28th of February, and took charge of one hundred wounded. Third, the Holland branch. This ambulance, under the direction of Dr. Candri, established itself in the Jewish school-house at first, afterward on the Esplanade. The effective was one of the best organized I have seen. Though small, it was complete, consisting of seven doctors of medicine and surgery, one pharmacien, and fifteen infirmiers. Their attention was principally given to forty-eight very severely wounded. They functioned from the 24th of November to the 1st of March. The people of Luxembourg also sent many valuable gifts, such as clothing, medicines, etc., also several of their surgeons. Thanks were later addressed by the municipal council, in the name of the city of Metz, to all these ambulances, for the devoted and conscientious fulfillment of the charitable mission they had undertaken. One or two of our officers have left, taking with them a *sauf-conduit* which the Prussians allow non-combatants. There is a general breaking-up. Marshal Bazaine set the example, by mounting in his *landau* and driving over to the headquarters of Prince Frederick Charles, where he dined. Dr. Good and myself begin to think about leaving and going to Dr. Lefort to obtain our discharges. The last thing we did in Metz was to steal a pig. On the Place St. Louis was an assemblage of marketers. Here several streets open; at the entrance to one of these was a wagon containing young pigs. This wagon had a bottom conisting of slats, and while the old woman in charge was engaged in striking a bargain with a French officer, one of them managed to squeeze through and make his his escape. We saw this and started up the street in pursuit: almost at the same moment another man also went after it, but observing us, said, "I suppose the pig is yours?" We answered, "Yes." He then stopped, and left us masters of the chase. Piggy turned a corner; but we soon overtook him, and drove him into a house, where we succeeded in capturing him. I took him by the hind legs and started off toward the "Black Eagle," —but by another way. The pig made such a squealing that everybody in the street came to the doors and windows; and we were finally obliged to get a sack, in which we put our prize, and I slung him across my shoulder: he was then quiet. That night we had pork chops, spare-ribs, sausages, etc.; and every one thought that the two Americans were very generous to spend their money on their comrades, who speculated on the price paid for the pig, which they said must have been very high.

October 31. Fair weather at last. All day yesterday and to-day Prussian troops, of different arms, are marching through Metz, *en route* for Paris. The conduct of the corps occupying Metz is, in every respect, praiseworthy. Our surgeons, etc., leave for Belgium by the evening train, the communications having been already re-opened to accommodate French officers going into Germany. The crowd is great that presses about the Prussian headquarters for *sauf-conduits*. Dr. Good and myself each obtain one for Tours; our intention being to join the Army of the Loire at that point, and serve out our time. The authorities who gave us this, informed us that we would not be able to arrive, and would certainly be arrested by the Prussian forces between Metz and Versailles, through which we were obliged to pass. However, we concluded to risk it.

November 1. A bright sunshine. At 6 A. M. we get up; take a hasty cup of coffee; strap our blankets behind our horses' saddles; put a comb, brush, and pocket-instruments, with some lint and bandages obtained from the Prussian medical department, into Good's saddle-bags; mount, and are off. As we passed the old Jardin Fabert, I could see all our wagons and material placed together in order, now the property of the German surgeons. We went out through the Porte de la France, crossed the river, and bore to the left, along the Verdun road. The villages that had been occupied by the Prussians, during the siege, were small fortresses in themselves. The empty barricades, loopholed houses, and trenches showed how well they had held their ground. Rising on the plain of Gravelotte we could obtain a good view of Metz, of the triple line of outworks, and places of German defense. We gave one farewell look at Metz, and then pressed forward. The plain was filled with huts, made of mud and the branches of trees: these the Prussian soldier occupies in time of war, when he does not happen to be quartered in a village. Tents are not used; the only ones they have are those taken from the enemy. We passed through Gravelotte. All about us was still and vacant. Two sentinels alone were there. On we rode. The fields were filled with graves. We soon saw another German soldier, crossing plowed ground to gain the main road, and join his column farther south. We stopped at midday, in a hamlet called Doncourt, where we rested for an hour. The first fresh beef that we tasted after the siege we got here. It made us both sick. We had some difficulty in getting hay and oats for our horses, but finally succeeded. That night, at 8 o'clock, we arrived in Étain, fifty miles west of Metz. Here we found M. Liégeois. He invited us to his house, where we spent a very pleasant night. This town was occupied by the Prussian Landwehr. Early next morning we were again on our way. The deep boom of a distant cannonade came to our ears as we sped along. It was the firing before Verdun, which was still being besieged. Presently we met a single company of Prussian soldiers resting by the roadside. We had several little amusing incidents during our day's ride, and arrived at evening in Dien, a village situated on a high hill, just opposite Verdun, and from which we could see the besiegers and the besieged. M. Liégeois had given us a letter to a friend of his, who entertained us, and told us many adventures he had had with the Prussians, who came after his sheep, wine, etc. He still had an officer quartered on him.

November 3. The roads are getting dry, and we are able to make good time. Nothing occurred worth noting, and we arrived, at dusk, in Clermont. As we drew up before the headquarters of the commandant de place, a crowd of soldiers gathered around us, and seemed surprised that we should be able to ride when we told them we just came from Metz. We got our *sauf-conduits* vised, and found a bed over a beer-saloon.

November 4. A clear, cold day. Our fears about our horses, that we had left during the night in charge of two Prussian soldiers, proved to be groundless. We leave Clermont, descending a slight declivity, our horses slipping on the frozen ground. At intervals we met trains of wagons, conducted by cavalry, who, upon perceiving us, would draw their swords, but, as we passed them, never attempted to use them. Reaching a narrow defile, we saw two German officers approaching us: they both drew their revolvers, and cocked them; which we appeared not to notice, leaving ours in our belts. These officers, holding their pistols in the hands nearest us, said, "Good-morning," as we neared them; and seeing that we did not show fight, appeared rather disappointed. We slept at Suippes that night.

The next morning was rather foggy; and as we rode along, we could hear voices near us, and just in advance. They proved to belong to a squad of Uhlans, who, on seeing us, barred the road with their crossed lances, and demanded our papers.

Toward evening we began to get on toward Rheims, the capital of Champagne. The country here was infested with guerrillas; and we deemed it advisable to dismount and lead our horses through a wood that was known to be filled with them, and that laid directly in our route. Nothing happened, and we arrived in Rheims. This city has from 50,000 to 75,000 inhabitants; the principal attractions being the magnificent cathedral and a few old Roman antiquities, including a triumphal arch of the time of Julius Cæsar. I must not forget to mention the champagne cellars of Widow Cliquot, which we visited. They are subterraneous, and three stories deep. Descending a long flight of stone steps, we arrive at the lowest room, which is devoted to large casks of wine, fresh from the grape; the second, or next above, is the bottling department, and on the first or highest floor the packing takes place. All three are connected by hatchways, and a railway runs the length of each, on which wine can be pushed back and forth. These cellars are 150 feet deep, and of immense length. We staid three days in Rheims, and got our papers vised.

November 9. We pursue our journey and pass the night at Charly.

November 10. The weather continues fair, and we meet with nothing worth noticing—except that we barely escaped being fired at. As we approached a sentinel, I by chance stopped to light my pipe, while Good rode on; my horse shied and turned around, as if to flee; the sentinel seeing this aimed at me, but Good put up his hand, and he did not fire. This occurred just outside of Gland, a village in the department of Marne. It was evening, and we drew up before an old inn. A few

French peasants were drinking in the café, as we entered and asked for a room. They gave us one on the first floor (the house was only one story high). We took our horses to the barn, which formed a part of the building, and being fatigued, retired immediately after supper.

CHAPTER XXIX.

The Murderous Attempt at Gland—We kill one and wound three—Flight in the Darkness—The two Villeneuves—Our Arrest—Chatenay—The Runaway—Arrival at Versailles—We give our Parole—Chartres.

ABOUT midnight we heard a noise as of some persons talking under our window. This was soon followed by the throwing of a stone and smashing of a pane. We jumped up, and hastily threw on our clothes: I took my revolver and went to the window. As soon as I appeared, a shot was fired; this I returned, and saw my man drop; Good came up and fired five shots in quick succession. The crowd seeing that we were well armed, dispersed; there was, in all, about a dozen of them. We had wounded three, and killed one; and now turned to the door in the determination to make our way to the stable. This we found locked, and were obliged to swing ourselves down the water-spout; I got down first; Good threw me out the saddle-bags, and followed. We found the stable-door likewise locked, and broke it open: it did not take us long to saddle and mount. As we were riding out of the stable-yard, two men sprang at our horses' heads: Good pricked spurs to his, and sent the man flying off; while I dealt mine a heavy blow over the head with the butt of my revolver, that threw him reeling to the ground. We dashed off into the darkness; one random shot was fired after us without effect. The secret of the whole disturbance was, that when he had entered the house early in the evening, our foreign accent had been remarked, and the inhabitants of the village had taken us for Prussian spies in French uniform. Their village being rather sequestered, and in the absence of all troops or authorities, they had doubtless intended to murder us. We did not halt until daylight, when we stopped at a farm-house and got breakfast. We passed the day on horseback, and got down for the night at La Ferté sous Jouarre.

November 12. All along our route we pass through villages where Prussian ambulances are established. We visited several of them, and found them full. The arrangements seemed exceedingly well made, and their discipline perfect. On one occasion I saw the infirmiers going through their evening drill. This the officer in charge told me was done in every ambulance throughout the German armies, to accustom the men to service on the field of battle as well as in the Lazarette. At Metz we never had a medical drill of any kind: outside they had two a day.

Here some of my notes fail, and I am obliged to skip; although I do not remember anything of interest having occurred until November 16.

We arrive at Boissy St. Leger, having passed through Meany and Château-Thierry. Boissy is situated on very high ground, about five miles south of Paris. We halted here at noon, and bought food of the Prussian sutlers: while we were there the army that passed through Metz on its way south, arrived. We left about 1 o'clock, and now began to follow around behind the German lines of siege, on the southern boundary of Paris, of which we could obtain a magnificent view: the dome of the Invalides, the Arc de Triomphe, and all the forts were before us. We could hear firing to the north. The road soon leaves this elevation, and descends to the Seine, crossing which, on a beautifully constructed war-bridge, we entered the village of Villeneuve St. George. It lies in a valley; was deserted and pillaged; some houses had been torn down, others burnt. In one that was comparatively well preserved, and had been, indeed, a handsome villa, I saw a flock of sheep in the first-story front, and a horse in the parlor. We did not stop here, but rode on to Villeneuve le Roi. This presented a great contrast to the village just named: everything was in order and occupied by Prussian soldiers and officers. I asked one of the latter, as we entered, if he could tell me where we could put up our horses: he recommended us to a large building which was then used as a cavalry barracks. We gave our horses in charge of one of the soldiers, and went out to seek quarters for the night.

We could find no accommodation anywhere, not even a place on the floor, and were about giving up in despair, when we were directed to a fine-looking mansion, above the gate of which floated the white flag and red cross. The building was situated about one hundred yards from the street, and before it spread a fine lawn. We entered, and were met, just inside, by Madame Ollivier, the proprietress. She received us with real French politeness, and informed us that only a few days previous some of our compatriots had come out from Paris, *en route* for England, and had given her a flying visit. She conducted Dr. Good into her house, where she said she was obliged to quarter the commander of the Prussian field-police. I remained behind, conversing with the gendarmes who had come up and demanded my papers. They examined them minutely: one of the two put them in his pocket; informed me that I was a prisoner, and told me to follow him.

We all three went into the house, and there found that

Good had likewise been arrested, and obliged to deliver up his papers. The four gendarmes withdrew, having first placed two guards under our window, which was on the ground floor. Madame Ollivier had assigned us a very pleasant room, and after giving us a nice supper, at which she herself presided, showed us to our apartment, and bid us good-night. We did not at all mind the sentinels outside, and slept soundly.

At 7 o'clock on the next morning, November 17, coffee was served us; and at half-past, a gentleman came to inform us that our horses were saddled and at the door.

We could not see Madame Ollivier to take leave, but left our cards and thanks on the dressing-table. We mounted and rode off, each having the company of a gendarme with drawn sword. We were soon out of Villeneuve, and cutting across the fields in the direction of Versailles, within range of the Paris outworks.

We had not gone far, when two of the very gendarmes that had arrested us the night before, dashed up, halted us, and asked our names; they compared those we gave now, with those we had given in Villeneuve; pronounced everything in order, and allowed us to proceed. Half an hour later, as we passed the corner of an old wall that lay in our way, the other two appeared and went through the same ceremony. At 12 o'clock we got out of the Prussian lines, and found ourselves among Bavarians, whose headquarters were at Chatenay. Thither we directed our course. The headquarters were, as usual, in the best house of the town. As soon as we had entered the yard, one of the two gendarmes that had accompanied us, dismounted and went in: presently an officer came out, and with great courtesy invited us to enter, saying that it would take some little time to arrange our papers. We accepted; he offered us seats, gave us a fine lunch, and made himself very agreeable.

After spending an hour with this gentleman, whose name was Lieutenant Von Hartmann, a secretary brought us our papers, and we rose to go. We found our horses in charge of two Bavarian cavalrymen, who told us they had been fed. We shook hands with the lieutenant, and started again. As we moved off at a walk, he shouted to the two horsemen, "Ride in front!" We were thus no longer regarded as prisoners, and had an escort all the way to Versailles. During this last stage of the journey, while endeavoring to ride lady-fashion for a short distance, my saddle slipped and sent me on the ground: my horse then became frightened, and ran away. One of the cavalrymen went in pursuit, and soon brought him back; the other aided me, somewhat bruised, to mount, and we proceeded on our way. It was 4 o'clock in the afternoon when we reached the Viroflay gate. From there we went to the Hôtel de France, fronting on the large Place d'Armes, in front of the palace. This vast space was now turned into an artillery park larger than any we had yet seen—having passed several on the road. We dismounted at the door of a small basement building in the court of the hotel: the escort gave our papers to a Prussian major, telling him that they had accompanied us, bid us adieu, and started back toward Chatenay. The major examined our passes, returned them, and told us we must speak to the general commander of Versailles, Von Voigts-Rhetz, to whom he conducted us. The general occupied a suite of rooms on the first floor of the hotel. After hearing our story, to which he listened with the closest attention, he said, "You must consider yourselves prisoners of war: give me your word of honor that you will not leave Versailles until peace is declared; if not, I shall be obliged to place you in confinement." We gave our parole, and he then told us that we were free. Our next care was to look for rooms; these we found at the Hôtel du Comte de Toulouse. Having received our month's pay in advance before leaving Metz, we felt pretty much at ease. In Versailles was established a French branch of the Sanitary Commission, subject to the orders of Prince Pless, commander of the volunteer medical corps of the German forces. We visited the French branch, and told them how our project of reaching the Army of the Loire had failed; further, that we wished to take service here. They gave us a letter of introduction to Prince Pless, whom we found residing in a splendid mansion on the Avenue de St. Cloud. His Highness regretted that he could do nothing for us.

November 18. We are at present gentlemen of leisure, and find it very hard work. A slight rain is falling, which has a dampening influence on our blue spirits. After breakfast we stroll over to the Hôtel des Reservoirs, and there find several of our compatriots, among others General Duff, military correspondent of the New York *Herald*, and Major McClean.

November 19. Time hangs heavily upon our hands. A few prisoners are brought in from the Paris army.

November 20. There is an inspection and search for arms in all the houses of Versailles. Having known that this was to take place, we confided our revolvers to the care of a friend, who was neutral, and thus preserved them. Our swords General Von Voigts-Rhetz had taken. We play billiards in the evening.

November 25. No change.

November 30. We are engaged writing.

December 1. The roar of the cannon shakes our windows at daybreak, announcing that the French are making a sortie: this comes from the heavy guns on Mont Valerien. It was the famous fight at Champigny, which lasted two days. The cold is intense. During this sortie, as, in fact, during all others, the gates of Versailles are closed, and cavalry, with drawn sabers, patrol the streets, while a battery at the head of each avenue is placed in position.

December 4. All quiet on the lines; several funerals of those who fell at Champigny take place, among others that of a French officer who had been wounded there and brought into Versailles a prisoner. The ceremony was held in the cathedral; most of the inhabitants attending. What struck me forcibly, was the large number of Prussian officers present, including General Von Voigts-Rhetz; he with others of his rank, walked behind the coffin of his fallen enemy who had only been a captain.

The next day we obtained a *sauf-conduit* to go to Chartres and bring back a horse belonging to Major McClean. We borrow a small wagon, to which we harness Dr. Good's horse, and start. The journey occupied ten hours; we stopped at Rambouillet for dinner, and there visited the château and park. We slept at Chartres. The cathedral in this town, which has 40,000 inhabitants and is situated in the department of Sisse, is singularly beautiful, and is built upon a subterranean church, to which you descend by torch-light. We returned to Versailles on the 6th of December.

CHAPTER XXX.

The Palace of Versailles turned into a Hospital—The Last Battle—Paris.

My task is nearly done; the rest is told in very few words. We remained in Versailles until the expiration of the term stipulated, making little excursions outside occasionally, to view the Prussian works of defense before Paris. We once succeeded in obtaining permission to take a three days' drive around the capital. This was very interesting, and we visited many ambulances.

When we returned to Versailles, having been unable to accomplish my object—viz., that of enlisting again in the field service—I joined the civil hospital, and there found enough to keep me busy, especially as at that time it was filled with French wounded. Dr. Ozanne was director. Frequent opportunity was afforded of visiting the grand Prussian military hospital, into which the palace had been turned. The elegant picture galleries and salons were filled with wounded. The German authorities had built up frames, extending from the ceiling to the floor, in front of the pictures and gilding, none of which were defaced or taken. This care of an enemy's property is, to say the least, praiseworthy. Dr. Busch very kindly showed me through his ward. The doctor had fifty beds consigned to him. He performed one visit at 8 o'clock in the morning, and a second at 3 in the afternoon, and had no assistants. Four infirmiers went with him from bed to bed. One carried a wooden frame, containing charpie, bandages, etc.; a second, a small light; a third, the irrigateur; the fourth man caried instruments.

Dr. Busch dressed every wound himself. He washed them with permanganate of potash, by means of Esmarch's irrigateur, and used no sponges. He claimed that the latter could never be kept entirely clean, and thus carried often infection to otherwise healthy wounds. He preferred to substitute a piece of fine linen.

On the 19th of January, the battle of Montretont took place; and on the 28th, Jules Favre, with Bismarck, signed the capitulation of Paris, where I succeeded in effecting my entrance the next day, disguised as Major McClean's servant. Peace was soon declared; but for a long time after, Paris presented the appearance of an immense hospital, and from nearly every other house hung the RED CROSS.

THE END.